I0824551

THE CREATIVE CONTAINER GARDEN

ANDERS RØYNEBERG
with Erik Schjerven

THE CREATIVE CONTAINER GARDEN

Grow a Vibrant, Year-Round Mix of Flowers, Food, Herbs, and More

TIMBER PRESS
Portland, Oregon

WELCOME TO BRANDBU

THE PLANTS AT BRANDBU

Project 1: Summer flowers

Project 2: Perennials and evergreens

Project 3: Ornamental grass

Project 4: Papyrus

Project 5: Vervain

Project 6: Bloom bonanza

Project 7: Sunflowers

Project 8: Popcorn grass

Project 9: Trees and shrubs

Project 10: Bulbs and tubers

Project 11: Cacti and succulents

Project 12: Tomatoes

Project 13: Potatoes

Project 14: Onions

Project 15: Herb garden

Project 16: Microgreens

Project 17: Mediterranean plants

GREENHOUSE DOME

RAINWATER COLLECTION

PLANTS KEPT INDOORS FOR WINTER

NETTLE WATER

ERIK HARVESTING VEGETABLES

LIQUID GOLD

GLASS GARDEN ROOM
Seeds and cultivation

DRY WELL

PLANTERS WITH CATNIP

CONCRETE TERRACE

STONE WALL

APPLE TREES

CORNFIELD

BERRY BUSHES

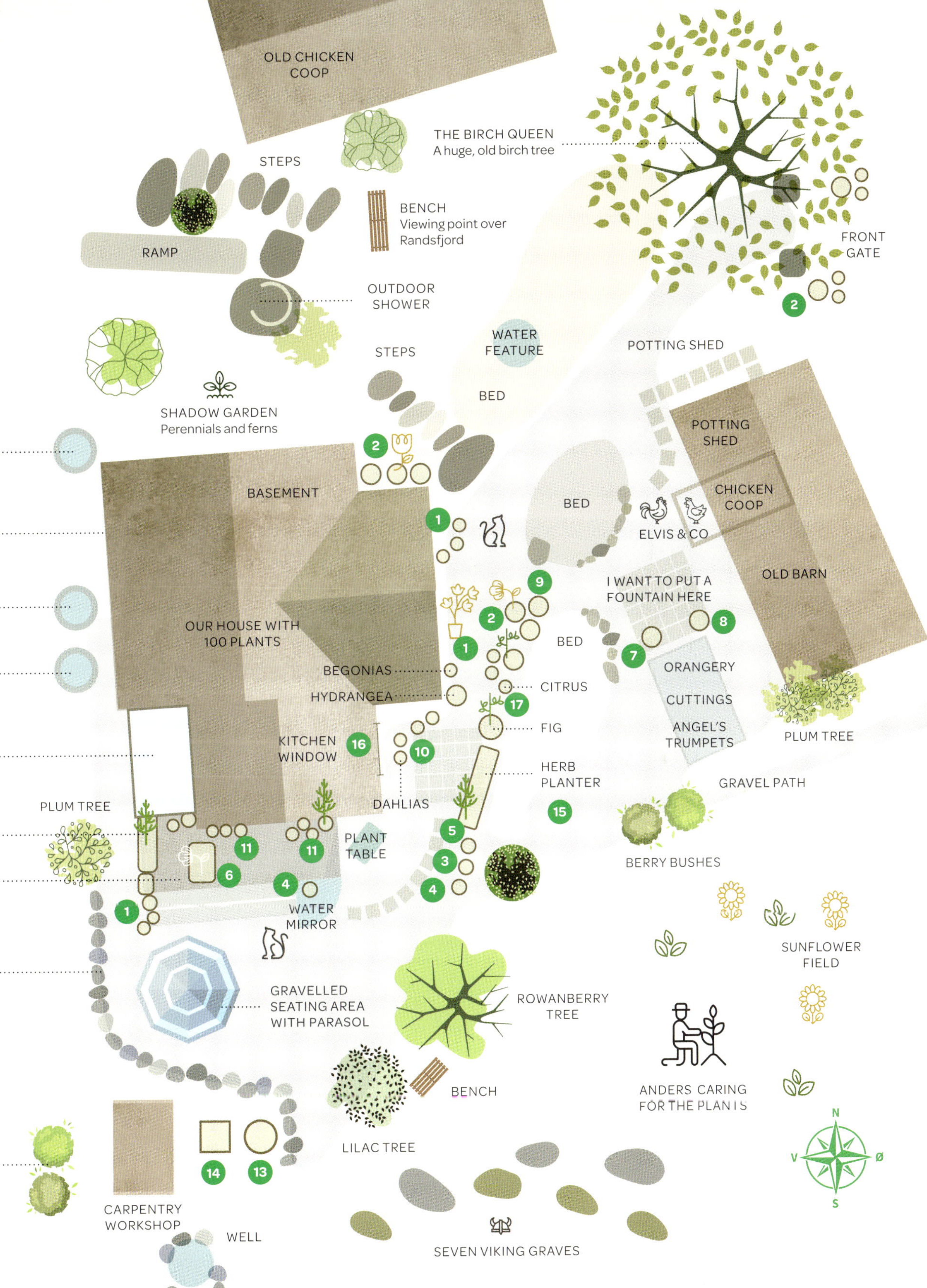
OLD CHICKEN COOP
THE BIRCH QUEEN
A huge, old birch tree
STEPS
BENCH
Viewing point over Randsfjord
RAMP
FRONT GATE
OUTDOOR SHOWER
2
WATER FEATURE
POTTING SHED
STEPS
BED
SHADOW GARDEN
Perennials and ferns
POTTING SHED
2
BASEMENT
CHICKEN COOP
BED
1
ELVIS & CO
9
I WANT TO PUT A FOUNTAIN HERE
OLD BARN
2
8
OUR HOUSE WITH 100 PLANTS
1
BED
7
BEGONIAS
ORANGERY
CITRUS
HYDRANGEA
CUTTINGS
17
ANGEL'S TRUMPETS
FIG
PLUM TREE
KITCHEN WINDOW
16
10
HERB PLANTER
GRAVEL PATH
DAHLIAS
15
PLUM TREE
PLANT TABLE
5
11
11
BERRY BUSHES
3
6
4
4
1
WATER MIRROR
SUNFLOWER FIELD
GRAVELLED SEATING AREA WITH PARASOL
ROWANBERRY TREE
BENCH
ANDERS CARING FOR THE PLANTS
N
V
Ø
S
LILAC TREE
14
13
CARPENTRY WORKSHOP
WELL
SEVEN VIKING GRAVES

It's not only about the life that you create in your pots, but the life around them: the people who can kick back and switch off, the birds, animals, and the bustling insect life. To the best land in the world: Hadeland—and to everyone here who has welcomed us with open arms!

CONTENTS

PREFACE
The Creative Container Garden

Being in a green outdoor space allows us to explore all of our senses. We can see, hear, smell, and sometimes taste, but we can also feel. A pot full of beautiful flowers spreads joy and provides us with positive sensory experiences. Is there anything more pleasant and enjoyable than spending time outside, surrounded by beautiful containers filled with summer flowers, herbs, edible plants, or ornamental trees? Not for me there isn't. A gorgeous container garden is simply plant-astic. It unleases my creative spirit.

Having a creative container garden means you'll have a stunning outdoor space, guaranteed to make you a little happier. You may find joy in new skills by nurturing your plants to sprout and grow. You can grow your own crops and harvest your own homegrown food. You may even improve your well-being, enjoy better health, and experience the therapeutic effects of tending to your garden.

I welcome you to my teeming universe of potted plants, where I share my top tips for how you can successfully cultivate your own outdoor containers, balcony boxes, and hanging baskets filled with your favorite plants. And if you don't have any favorites yet, I have lots of tips and ideas that I hope you'll be inspired by.

Do you want a container garden bursting with flowers, trees, perennials, herbs, and tomatoes? This book is for anyone who is looking to learn how to succeed with potted plants, find inspiration for what you can grow in containers, gain insight into how to care for your plants, and, not least, understand how to make them thrive and look their best.

You don't need hundreds of containers, by the way—you can learn how to make the most out of your outdoor space with just a few. Perhaps you feel you have a black thumb because you've killed a few potted plants? Then that makes two of us. Succeeding with plants is a matter of trial and error, with ups and downs along the way. Basic knowledge of each plant's needs, along with the fact that practice makes perfect, ensures that you will eventually find plant care to be easier and more enjoyable for all your plants. If I can do it, so can you.

There's almost no limit to what you can grow in your outdoor pots—everything from beautiful ornamental shrubs to edible plants such as herbs and vegetables. I hope you find this book engaging and inspiring, and I wish you well on your creative journey.

Happy reading and happy planting!

INTRODUCTION

Guess which floor I lived on? If you live in a city with a balcony or courtyard, there are opportunities to grow your own plants in pots and boxes. This was the balcony of my apartment in Oslo. The climbing plants on the wall are different types of perennial clematis, which thrive in large pots. The balcony boxes feature a mixture of ivy, lavender, lobelia, petunias, and a small fan palm. Over time, I noticed that more and more of my neighbors had more and more balcony plants.

Our senses have developed such that the closer something is to us, the stronger an impression it makes. A great outdoor space encourages us to take a break and really see the small details around us. Have you noticed the beautiful flowers just starting to sprout, or the hundreds of insects that visit your potted plants throughout the day?

Create Your Own Oasis

I have lived high and low in both the city and the countryside. I've gone from apartment living with a small balcony and just a few container plants to now having a farm with an expansive garden and space for plenty of pots.

It doesn't matter where you start. Whether you live in an urban area with a balcony and courtyard or in the countryside with a garden and terrace, you can create your own container garden. The advantage of containers is that they don't require much space, and that you can grow whatever plants you want. Containers can be easily moved around, and in so doing they can create atmosphere and transform your outdoor area into a beautiful oasis where people, animals, and insects can all thrive.

In this book, I'll give you an introduction to growing indoor and outdoor container plants, simple suggestions for good choices for your pots and plants, specific tips on how to succeed with your plants, and lots of creative ideas for container garden projects that you can easily enjoy in your outdoor space, regardless of its size.

I'll dig into everything from standard pots to long planters, exploring the various forms of soil-filled containers suitable for a smaller outdoor space. For the sake of simplicity, I'll refer to most of these vessels as "containers," including balcony boxes, raised beds, planters, and the like.

The plant world is enormous, with hundreds of thousands of different plants from which to choose. That's why I've recommended the plants that I personally like and have succeeded with, so that you can choose yourself from a tried and tested selection of plants.

Container gardening is contagious, just so you know. You might risk becoming rather popular around the neighborhood if you beautify your area with potted plants. Everyone enjoys having something pretty to look at, and it's always nice to spread some floral joy.

The genius of containers is that you can use them indoors, on the balcony, on the terrace, or in the garden, regardless of whether you have a large or small space. Here is a fig tree on my balcony in Oslo. Figs: see page 252.

THE MANY ADVANTAGES OF OUTDOOR CONTAINERS

- Require little space.
- Beautify your outdoor space.
- Can be placed exactly where you want.
- Creative expression: pots become part of your interior design outside.
- Zero to minimal weeding.
- You can grow your favorite crop without competing with weeds.
- Easy to move indoors for the winter if necessary.
- Adds vibrancy to your outdoor space with a huge variety of color options, types of pot, and sizes.
- Easy accessibility—pots with herbs, for example, can be placed near the kitchen and other cooking areas.
- Earlier germination as potting soil is heated faster by the spring sun than soil in the ground.

Containers can easily be placed wherever you want your plants to live, whether that's on a balcony, a terrace, in a courtyard, by the front door, in the garden, or in any other outdoor space.

Keep a Close Eye

Plants in containers may require more care and supervision in the form of watering and fertilizer and are more exposed to the effects of frost and wind. This depends entirely on the type of containers you use. Small pots will require more frequent watering, simply because they hold less soil, which will then dry out more easily. Placing your containers in a particularly sunny spot will also lead to the soil drying out faster. Plastic pots will retain moisture better than clay pots. I have several good preventative tips for this, which I'll discuss later on in the chapter.

Plant joy: Looking at flowers makes me happy, growing flowers makes me happy, talking about flowers makes me happy, picking flowers makes me happy, seeing plant-loving people talking enthusiastically about their plants makes me happy.

When I met Erik, I asked if he would like to come home and look at my plants, a well-known checkbox among plant lovers. And it worked. Plants bring people together.

Erik was a plant serial killer when I met him. Sometimes I still shoot him a stern look when he's careless with the plants, waters them too aggressively with the garden hose, or forgets to water one of the pots on the patio, even though he was told to water ALL of them. Perhaps it's a sign of being a bit of a control freak, but these plants are living beings, after all. Right, Erik?

Calamondin tree

Plants Do Us Good

Research shows that plants can help improve our health. When we see flowers, dopamine is released in the body, making us happy and less stressed. Being surrounded by thriving plants simply makes us feel that much better. So it's beneficial, this contagious creativity.

Containers Can Go Anywhere

Do you need a garden with soil to cultivate? Not at all—pots can be placed on a balcony, terrace, veranda, or by the front door. They can sit on gravel, cement, stone, tiles, and various other places where there is no soil. So there's no excuse not to have a pot or ten.

Practice Makes Perfect

It's a terrible feeling when one of your plants dies, but it's happened to all of us. It's okay to feel that gardening and cultivating plants are frustrating and difficult at times, but don't give up. Look at the small missteps as valuable experiences to learn from. Plant care gets easier and more enjoyable with time, practice, and patience.

It feels wonderful when your potted plants are flourishing, blooming, and looking healthy. My first book was called *Green Home* and was precisely about the fact that plants provide an opportunity for us to gain new skills, make us feel great, and can create a feeling of #plantpride.

But what if the opposite happens? What if your plant dies? It's awful when this occurs and can undermine your confidence. I think that because plants are living organisms, we feel extra sad when they die. They require care and nurturing. It makes them mortal—some grow and some die. Such is life, including plant life. It is important to be aware that some plants do, genetically, have a shorter lifespan, while others can live and become as old

From a small balcony in the city to a house with a large outdoor space. The beautiful thing about pots is that you can create your mini garden regardless of the size of your space. Erik and I now live on a small farm in Brandbu, in an area of southeastern Norway called Hadeland, with our cats Juni and Juli, our hens Bianca, Bruna, Thelma, and Louise, and our rooster Elvis. Here we have a large outdoor space with plenty of pots and opportunities to sow and grow.

CONTAINER TIP

How about planting summer flowers together in a larger pot? Here, you can see a combination with cosmos and dahlias, planted in an old rusty oil barrel. For this one, I put the tallest ones (the cosmos) at the back and the smaller flowers (the dahlias) at the front to create a kind of wave effect that starts at the bottom and moves upwards.

as, or even older than, us humans. Plant care is all about experience, so we don't need to focus so much on our mistakes. The most important thing is not to give up, and to understand that practice makes perfect—regardless of whether you are a top athlete, chef, seamstress, prime minister, or, like us, balcony farmers and plant lovers.

With a background as a nurse, I know the importance of preventing injury and illness. Read more about how you can cultivate healthy and beautiful plants in the chapter on care on page 59.

GARDENING FOR HEALTH

Contact with plants has a major impact on your health. More and more research shows that twenty minutes engaged in some form of contact with nature (such as tending to your potted plants) reduces stress (cortisol) levels in the body. The best thing is that you don't have to be in the middle of a national park to experience nature. You can give your body a dose of nature wherever you are. Those who have access to some form of garden and outdoor space report greater well-being, better health, and more physical activity.

You shouldn't skimp on the small moments to enjoy nature that everyday life offers, whether that may be enjoying the sight of cut flowers in a vase, watering your balcony plants, or spending time in a park or other lush outdoor space. Every little bit helps. The more time you spend with nature, the better.

Why not plant some herbs or vegetables of your own in your pots? We were created to be close to nature, but in today's society most of us live cut off from exactly what we need to feel good. Bring nature into your home, and experience the benefits of a green home environment.

If a flamboyant person were a flower, they would be the splash of color that is the begonia. And if you are a flamboyant person reading this, that's meant as a *big* compliment.

CONTAINER TIP
Make Your Containers Accessible

It's a good idea to have your potted plants as close and accessible as possible. If you place them in areas you pass often, and where you like to spend your time, it's easier to keep an eye on them and give them the right care. You'll get more pleasure from them. I have several planters and boxes that I placed a little too far away in my garden, and they are unfortunately overgrown and neglected every year. The herb pots at the kitchen entrance, on the other hand, are used extensively for cooking every summer. It only takes us a couple of minutes to pop outside and harvest some herbs, and then put them straight into our meal. Accessibility is key!

Growing up, I felt different and weird. I was queer and unlike the others in the Christian missionary environment I grew up in. I continued to feel like I didn't fit in, and eventually started thinking that there was something wrong with me, almost as if I were some kind of weed. During this period, it did me a world of good to be outside, connecting with plants and nature—a lifesaver, even. I would spend hours among the trees and flowers. I often lay in the green grass, gazing up at the sky and thinking deep tween thoughts, as deep as tween thoughts can be anyway. I had my dog Max by my side too, a really good friend with one brown and one blue eye, who constantly looked at me and looked after me, in return for a small pat or treat.

The Diversity of Plants

Plants are diverse, and so are people—thank goodness.

Have you ever felt like a bit of an oddball, like you don't fit in? Like you're different and don't belong anywhere? Do as I do and be inspired by the diversity of the plant world. Perhaps you're like the dahlia, which takes up the space around it with its extravagant and pompous flowers. Or maybe you're more like the slender, modest, and mellow lavender, the robust and hardy succulents, or perhaps you're more like the sweet and charming tomato? A tutti-frutti flower bouquet is all about its beautiful diversity, with its myriad appearances, strengths, and characteristics. Just think how boring the world would be if we were all the same.

"Hurrah for the diversity of nature, of plants and people."

Throughout the summer, you will also be able to experience the flutter of butterflies and other insects enjoying your container garden as much as you do. Maybe the bumblebee that keeps visiting your flowers has also got a case of container garden fever? All of a sudden you're surrounded by wonderful nature, by plant and insect life in your own home.

CHAPTER 1

CHOOSING YOUR PLANTS AND POTS

Allium, in this case black garlic (*A. nigrum*), is a genus of bulbous plant that produces large round balls of flowers that often tower over other flowers. They are eye-catching, perennial, and a favorite with the bumblebee. In other words, this plant is a good choice for those who like easy-to-care-for potted plants.

What to Know Before Getting Started

The range of plants to choose from is enormous, and some may find it difficult to narrow down the options and navigate the sea of plant varieties. Even I, who have been tinkering with pots and plants since I was young, think it can be rather challenging and complicated at times. But above all, it's exciting and fun, and I love experimenting with new plants and things to grow, not least because it nurtures my container garden obsession. Let the fever run wild and challenge yourself to try something new.

I personally like having everything from annual flowers to perennials and evergreens. Also relevant here are hardiness zones (see page 36).

Here's a brief overview of the different categories of potted plants and some tips on what you can fill your plant pots with:

Annual flowers are planted for one season with the aim of a beautiful floral display. These die when the frost comes. The marguerite daisy (*Argyranthemum* spp.) (on page 33, top) is an example.

Perennials are plants that enter a dormant period when the frost comes, and will hopefully peek out of their pots again when the spring sun returns, if properly overwintered. The hosta (*Hosta* spp.) (see photo, bottom left) is a perennial, as is the clematis (*Clematis* spp.) (photo bottom right).

Exotic plants is a broad category, but I use it for shrubs and small trees indigenous to hot climates, like the Mediterranean. These plants cannot withstand frost and must therefore be kept indoors through the winter. Examples include all sorts of citrus trees (*Citrus* spp.), figs (*Ficus carica*), and olive trees (*Olea europaea*).

"Humankind is like a pot of flowers, some sprout and grow, others burst into full bloom, while others fade and wither."

Seeds. Many plants can be sown as seeds in the spring and will sprout when watered and the soil temperature rises. Examples of these are sunflowers (*Helianthus annuus*), fiddleneck (*Phacelia tanacetifolia*), and poppies (*Papaver* spp.).

Tuberous plants are those that grow from thickened underground stems that contain the nutrients necessary to send out shoots for new plants and sustain them. Some tubers are not cold-hardy and will need to be dug up at the end of the season and kept dry and frost-free over the winter, to be planted again when there is no longer any danger of frost. These include dahlias and some types of begonias. Potatoes (*Solanum tuberosum*) are also tubers.

Bulbs also store nutrients necessary for new growth and that sustain the plant when it is dormant. Many bulbs are cold-hardy and can remain in the ground through the winter. Tulips (*Tulipa* spp.) are perhaps the best-known flowering bulb, but there are many others, such as grape hyacinth (*Muscari* spp.), daffodils (*Narcissus* spp.), and spring squill (*Scilla vernum*).

The plant universe is extensive, so I recommend you take a deep breath and maintain the mindset that you'll be learning along the way. You can choose the same plants to tend to year after year or experiment with new ones each season. See it as a learning and development opportunity, and advance when you feel ready.

Marguerite daisies (page 156) are a good choice for annual summer flowers. They are versatile and bloom throughout the season. If you pluck off any spent flowers (deadhead) a few times during the growing period, you will be rewarded with new buds and a rich abundance of blossoms.

CONTAINER TIP

You can make life much easier for yourself by buying flowers already in bloom that you can plant directly outside. You don't *have* to sow the seeds yourself or wait for bulbs or tubers to sprout and blossom. Cheating? Absolutely not. Buy your plants from a local nursery and talented professionals, and support a gardener who has spent time growing the plants that you get to enjoy and care for.

ASK YOURSELF, BEFORE GETTING STARTED

Smart questions to ask yourself before getting started on your potted garden:

Time

Do I want easy-to-care-for plants, or do I have the capacity for plants that need more supervision and maintanence?

Plant Choice

Will I be happy with just summer annuals that need to be replanted each year, or do I want perennials that can remain in their pots and will come back year after year?

Space

Does my outdoor space allow for large plants and trees, or is it better to have smaller ones? Do I need to move my potted plants indoors during the winter, and, if yes, do I have space inside to do so?

Cost

How much money can I spend? Can I invest in pots and plants, or do I want a budget-friendly container garden? Do I want to invest a lot now, or do I want to build it up over time?

Climate

What plants will thrive and grow in the weather conditions where I live? If I choose perennials, can they survive the winter outdoors, or should they be brought indoors? Does it rain a lot or a little in the summer, and how strong a wind can they withstand? How often do we experience frost and subzero temperatures in the winter?

Dahlias—my favorite flower purchase. They were in full bloom from May all the way through to October.

The Zones—What and Why?

If you want to succeed with your potted perennials, it's good to know what a hardiness zone is. This means the zone you live in, and the zone the plant can tolerate and in which it can survive winter.

FIND YOUR HARDINESS ZONE

The USDA Plant Hardiness Map is divided into zones 1a through 13b, which are determined by the average lowest minimum temperature experienced in that area over the past thirty years. The lower the number of the zone you live in, the more mindful you must be when choosing plants if you want them to survive year after year, because of the degree of cold they may be exposed to. In this book, I've tried to include particularly cold-hardy plants so that no matter where you live, you can help your potted plants thrive.

The hardiness zone with the mildest climate is 13b, with an average low temperature of 65° to 70°F/18.3° to 21.1°C, while the coldest is 1a, with an average extreme minimum temperature of −60° to −55°F/−51.1° to −48.3°C.

You can find which hardiness zone you live in at planthardiness.ars.usda.gov by popping in your zip code.

Here at Brandbu, we have cold winters with snow and regularly experience subzero temperatures. Because of this, I choose fairly robust plants with a high level of hardiness for my pots. You can usually find the hardiness zone of a plant marked on its label.

Suggestions for perennials and evergreens with a high degree of cold hardiness:

Smaller Plants

- Hostas
- Ferns (cold-tolerant species like *Matteuccia struthiopteris* and *Dryopteris filix-mas*)
- Catnip (*Nepeta cataria*)
- Coral bells (*Heuchera sanguinea*)
- Astilbe (*Astilbe*)
- Common columbine (*Aquilegia vulgaris*)
- Breckland thyme (*Thymus serpyllum*)

Larger Plants

- Rhododendron (*Rhododendron* spp.)
- Chinese peony (*Paeonia lactiflora*)
- Common hop (*Humulus lupulus*)
- Purple clematis (*Clematis viticella*)
- Black chokeberry (*Aronia melanocarpa*)
- Dwarf mountain pine (*Pinus mugo*)
- White spruce (*Picea glauca*)

CONTAINER TIP

Potted plants are more exposed to cold winds and freezing temperatures than those planted in the ground, which are protected by the soil. Pots, on the other hand, can turn into small freezers in the cold. For that reason, it's wise to choose plants that are even more cold-hardy than the zone you live in. For instance, if you live in Zone 7a, with an average extreme minimum temperature of 0° to 5°F/–17.8° to –15°C, look for plants that can thrive in Zone 6a, with a minimum temperature of –10° to –5°F/–23.3° to –20.6°C.

These potted perennials, consisting mostly of ferns and hostas, can remain outside over the winter, but need to be sheltered, such as against a wall. This increases their chance of survival. In this photo, they are sprouting again after being dormant through the winter.

CONTAINER TIP

Always check the USDA zone when buying a plant; it can vary within the same genus and plant family.

Annual Flowers and Hardiness Zones

If you opt for annual flowers that cannot survive the winter, the hardiness zone isn't that important. The only thing to keep in mind is that annuals cannot withstand frost, so be careful when setting out seedlings, as frosty nights may occur in the spring. Most annuals will continue to bloom right up until the frost comes in the fall, when they will wither and die.

Perennials and Hardiness

If you're looking for plants that return year after year, you're best off choosing a perennial. Here, however, it is important to know which hardiness zone you live in, and which hardiness zone the plant can withstand. It is such a pity when you see plants freeze to death, so make sure to choose robust plants that can survive the winter where you live.

Can You Influence the Hardiness Zone Where You Live?

Yes, absolutely. By creating a zone with more shelter in your outdoor space, for example by placing pots and planters up against a warm wall, in a sunny corner, or behind larger trees and bushes that help shield the plants from the wind, you will be able to protect them and make the environment somewhat milder.

Planters are practical and beautiful, and they create sheltered zones with less wind. Here, containers find protection from the wind.

The three most common types of pots are untreated clay pots, glazed clay pots, and plastic pots.

Personally, I'm most fond of pots made of terra-cotta or glazed ceramic. For plants that love the sun and can withstand dry soil, such as succulents and cacti, I opt for terra-cotta. For plants that need more water and consistent access to water and moisture, glazed ceramic or plastic pots are my preferred choice.

Choosing a Pot

Most pots on the market are made of the following materials:

- Ceramic
- Terra-cotta, earthenware
- Stoneware
- Concrete
- Composite materials (fiberglass, etc.)
- Plastic

You can find all sorts of different pots, and what your pot is made of can actually have consequences for your plant's growth and well-being.

Basically, you can use whichever type of pot you prefer or can afford, but the most common varieties have their advantages and disadvantages.

Clay pots, often referred to as terra-cotta pots, are both attractive and suitable for plants that like the soil to absorb water faster, such as lavender, geraniums, catnip, grass, and herbs. You do then have to water the plant more frequently,

A budget-friendly container garden—plastic mortar buckets filled with soil. Remember to drill holes in the bottom, so that any excess water can escape; this will result in healthier roots and happier plants.

because the clay itself absorbs a lot of water, but you will often be rewarded with healthier roots and thriving plants.

It is difficult to find the right balance with small clay pots, as they dry out quickly and need to be watered a lot more often. Small plants can therefore benefit from being planted in plastic pots, which better retain moisture. You can also use a plastic pot to plant in, and then put the plastic pot inside a pot made of another material to hide it, especially if you're looking to create a certain aesthetic in your container garden.

Glazed pots are clay pots with a coating and are often colorful, beautiful, and a bit more expensive. They breathe less and better retain moisture than their popular terra-cotta counterparts.

Plastic pots are cheap, easy to move, and retain moisture well. This type of pot is suitable if you want smaller potted plants and would prefer not to have to water your plants as often. They are therefore ideal for plants that like the soil to stay moist, such as hostas, ferns, dahlias, and begonias. Plastic mortar tubs are reasonably priced, come in various sizes, and can be handy for planting in. I think there's something humble and unassuming about plants in plastic tubs and buckets.

CONTAINER TIP

If it's windy or your potted plants grow tall and are in danger of toppling over, pots made of heavier materials, such as cement, steel, or glazed terra-cotta, are particularly handy. Alternatively, you can fill the bottom of the pot with small stones, gravel, or sand. If you want larger pots that are easier to move, choose pots made from plaster or fiberglass.

Balcony boxes are most commonly made of plastic, as they retain moisture, are light, and can easily be lifted and attached to railings. Just remember to fasten them securely to the railing or edge if you decide to hang them up.

Size Matters

When planting in pots, the larger the pot, the more likely you are to succeed. Large pots hold more soil, and more soil retains water and nutrients better, which the plants need to thrive. In small pots, the soil dries out more easily, which often causes the plant to wither and die. But remember, if you plant a tiny plant in a huge pot, there may then be *too much* soil and moisture, which will keep the roots from thriving.

I personally prefer pots and planters with a diameter of 12 inches/30 cm or larger. I generally increase the size of the pot gradually if the plant gets too big. If necessary, you can trim the plants so that they don't grow too large. If space is limited, go for fewer, larger pots rather than lots of smaller pots. The smaller ones are more challenging, as the plants require more frequent care and watering. It's therefore easier for us with container garden fever to have large pots with plenty of opportunities for planting. This gives me more time to enjoy the sight of my lush potted garden as I don't have to water them as often.

CONTAINER TIP

Pots made of plastic, aerated concrete, or fiberglass are easier to move around, as they weigh less. If you have heavier pots, it might be a good idea to invest in a hand truck, or find a friend with big biceps.

Raised beds and planters are usually made of wooden materials that can be easily put together and assembled yourself, or otherwise bought ready-made in wood or steel. The latter are beautiful and solid, but are often a bit more expensive.

Frost-Proof Pots Are a Good Investment

If you have pots that will be left outside during the winter, you must make sure that these are frost-proof. Ask if the pots are frost-proof when purchasing, so you know your plants won't be killed off over the winter. It is also smart to leave your pots standing on pot feet, or wooden or polystyrene blocks, so that they avoid any frost from undenreath, and it keeps them from freezing to the ground. Raising pots off the ground also ensures good drainage. You should check that the potting soil doesn't get too wet in late fall, just before the frost arrives. You can move the pots closer to the wall of your home, or under the shelter of a roof to protect them from the rain. This will reduce the likelihood of any harmful frost cracking your pots.

SUMMARY OF CHAPTER 1

Choosing Your Plants and Pots

- Select plants that suit your experience level and location. You can choose from annual summer flowers, perennials, exotic plants, tuberous plants, and bulbs.
- Understanding your hardiness zone is a good idea when it comes to choosing plants that can thrive in your area. This allows you to plan your container garden accordingly.
- The material your pots are made of matters. The type of pot you choose affects the well-being of your plants, and different types of plants have different preferences.
- Large pots provide better water and nutrient conditions, while small pots can result in your soil drying out and poor growth.
- If you plan to keep your pots outside over the winter, it is important to choose frost-proof pots and to raise them above the ground to avoid frost damage.

CHAPTER 2

PLANTING IN POTS

This homegrown coleus that I cultivated from a cutting (see page 84) is ready to be repotted into a larger container filled with fresh new nutrient-rich soil.

I've got container garden fever! Is there anything more joyous and satisfying than creating your own potted garden with summer flowers, herbs, edible plants, or ornamental trees? In this chapter, you'll find tips and tricks on how to succeed with potted plants in your outdoor space.

A Step-by-Step Guide

New plant, new pot. After you have chosen the right plants and pots to suit you and your climate, the time has come for the actual planting. Direct repotting into a larger pot is a good idea for newly acquired plants. I recommend this, because the plant will want new nutrient-rich soil and more space for its roots. If you're good with new plants, whether you've grown them yourself, bought them at a nursery, or been given them as a gift, this will give the plants a fresh start right away, with a bigger pot and new, healthy soil.

Repotting Your Plant

What You'll Need

- A new pot
- Nutrient-rich soil
- A watering can

What I Recommend

- Drainage aids (sand, gravel, LECA, perlite)
- Drainage hole(s) in the bottom of the pot
- Saucer

Additional Equipment That Might Be Useful

- Support stakes
- Plant food
- Pruning shears

These pea shoots are thriving, but, as you can see, the roots are looking for more space and soil—in other words, they want a bigger pot.

CONTAINER TIP

Are the roots of your plant poking out through the drainage holes? This means that the plant's roots are in search of more space and nutrition—a sign that the plant needs a bigger pot and new soil.

For the sake of simplicity, you can, of course, just keep the plant in the pot it comes in. But if you want to provide your plant with the best conditions, give it a slightly larger pot and fresh soil, so that it reaches its full potential and your potted garden can be as lush as possible. And that's exactly what I want to do with this book: to spread my container garden fever so that you too can create your own oasis.

How Big a Pot Do I Need?

Feel free to double the size of the pot when repotting. If the pot is 6 inches/15 cm in diameter, repot your plant in a 12-inch/30-cm pot. The size obviously depends on the plant's needs to a certain extent too: plants that grow fast and have a lot of flowers, such as dahlias will often require more space.

You can get even bigger pots for these, such as something with a 16-inch/40-cm diameter. Plants that grow more slowly and don't need as much nutrient-rich soil, such as succulents and Mediterranean herbs like lavender (*Lavandula* spp.), sage (*Salvia* spp.), and catnip (*Nepeta cataria*), can thrive when their roots are packed in tightly and require less frequent repotting.

What Kind of Soil Should I Use?

You'll go a long way with good soil formulated for flowers, which is suitable for most plants. Cheaper potting soil is often of poorer quality and contains less nutrition. Otherwise, there are lots of affordable and good compost soil options available. See pages 74 through 81 for more detailed information.

A Step-by-Step Guide to Planting in Pots

1. Let the potting soil around the new plant soak through before you place it into the new pot. This prevents the soil clod from drying out. Use a watering can or submerge the entire pot in a bucket of water, and let the plant soak up all the water it needs for a few minutes.

2. Gently squeeze the outside of the plastic pot and loosen the clod of soil. Feel free to lay it on its side: gravity will help and it will be easier to wiggle the plant loose.

3. Free the plant from the pot by shimmying it out, along with the clod of soil. Be careful not to pull too hard on the stem or foliage, as the plant may break away from the roots. Try to ease the plant from the pot without pulling too much. Use your fingers or a small spade to loosen the clod of soil—this will make things much easier.

4. Consider removing some of the old soil, as the plant has often eaten up most of the nutrients in it.

5. Tousle the roots a little from the base. You do this to remove old soil, as well as to free the roots so that they can quickly settle into the new potting soil and get a good start.

6. Place the drainage aids in the bottom of the new pot. This should come to about 1 to 2 inches/3 to 5 cm deep at the bottom of the pot, so a couple of handfuls should do. You can use LECA, pebbles, or sand. LECA makes for slightly lighter pots, while pebbles and sand make the pots heavier and more stable—a smart choice if the pots are exposed to the wind.

7. Pour the soil over the drainage aids. As a rule, you should put enough soil in until it fills about one-third of the pot.

8. Check that the clod of soil fits into the new pot and on top of the new soil. Keep in mind that the soil clod should be covered with about an inch of soil at the top of the new pot.

9. Place the plant and the clod of soil in the pot and top up with new soil around it.

10. Check that the plant is level and centered in the middle of the pot. It's often useful to have a helping hand here, so that one person can keep the plant in the center and the other can fill the pot with soil.

11. Top up the pot with plenty of soil, potentially even mixing in some drainage material along the way, so that the final ratio is preferably about one-quarter drainage material and three-quarters soil.

12. Push the plant down and into place steadily and with firm pressure, but without using too much force. If the roots are squeezed together too much, this may be detrimental to the plant.

13. Water the soil thoroughly, preferably until a little water runs out through the drainage hole(s) at the base of the pot.

14. Now it's time to place the pot wherever you want, but remember that most plants like to get at least a few hours of direct sunlight. The length of time each plant does best spent in the sun varies from plant type to plant type. Hostas and ferns do well in the shade, while lavender, sage, and catnip prefer a lot of sun.

Ta-da, you're done! Take a step back and enjoy the sight of your beautiful new potted plant!

The next thing you'll need to know is what kind of care the plant needs to thrive, all of which you can find in chapter 3 on caring for your potted plants.

Drainage materials—use LECA, sand, or simply gravel from your driveway.

CONTAINER TIPS

Some Advice

Drainage Holes in the Base

Ensuring there are holes in the bottoms of your pots is a must for draining excess water. If the pot is tightly packed, excess water won't be able to drain out and the soil will end up sitting in water over time. The plant's roots will eventually rot, and the plant may become sick and die, otherwise known as root rot. If you don't already have a hole in the bottom of your pot, you can make one or more by using a drill. Using a diamond bit in the drill will help on tougher materials.

Drainage Aids

By mixing drainage aids like sand, gravel, or LECA into the soil, you are making the soil lighter and more breathable. This means the plant's roots are more likely to thrive, and you'll have a healthier plant. I use one-quarter drainage aids and three-quarters soil.

Gravel, sand, and LECA are good products for ensuring more breathable soil in which roots can thrive.

Plant Deep Enough

Make sure that your newly planted soil clod doesn't sit above the soil layer in the new pot. If it does, the plant will suffer, the roots will become sick, and, in the worst case scenario, the plant will die. Cover the clod well with new soil, approximately 1 to 2 inches/3 to 5 cm.

Gardening on a Budget?

Looking to ensure good drainage without spending a lot of money? You probably already have things in your home that you can use.

Fill the pot a quarter full with organic material like twigs, leaves, or, as shown in the photo below, corks from wine and champagne bottles (made of natural cork) before filling the pot the rest of the way full with soil. Doing this ensures you are adding nutrients, making the soil more breathable, and reusing organic material. Cheap and sustainable!

One of the most relaxing things for me is repotting my plants. It fills me with so much joy to give the plants a bit of love and care and then be rewarded with lush, abundant growth. It's no wonder I have container garden fever!

CHAPTER 2 SUMMARY

Planting in Pots

- New plant, new pot: I recommend repotting your plant in a larger container to ensure fresh growth. That way, you can give your plant new nutrient-rich soil and more space.
- Equipment required: a new pot, nutrient-rich soil, drainage aids, and a watering can.
- Double the pot size when repotting. Based on my own experience, this ensures healthy and robust plants.
- Remember to thoroughly water the plant before repotting to avoid any drying out.
- Place the drainage aids at the bottom of the new pot to ensure healthy roots.

CHAPTER 3

CARING FOR YOUR CONTAINER PLANTS

It is a common misconception that caring for a container garden is difficult and time-intensive, but the truth is that you can go a long way with just a little knowledge, a few solid routines, and a healthy dose of enthusiasm. If you know a little about light, temperature, water, and nutrition, there is a high probability that you'll be rewarded with a garden of lush plants and catch a case of container garden fever as well.

Plant Care, Soil, Fertilizer, and Maintenance

"What's the secret to getting healthy potted plants?" is a question I'm often asked. In short, plants thrive best when they have regular access to water, nutrient-rich soil topped off with a supply of plant food, and regular attention. It sounds simple enough, but it does still feel like an art to master, even for those who have long since been bitten by the potted plant bug.

"Growing in pots often gives you greater control over the soil, nutrient supply, and water for each individual plant than if they were planted in a bed, where the plants compete with each other and some disappear."

Succulents and cacti (opposite) are examples of plants that like it sunny, dry, and sandy, with barren soil, just like it is where they come from: the desert.

With my background as a nurse, I am always focused on providing good care. The best for everyone is, of course, preventive treatment, to avoid getting sick in the first place. In a plant context, this means giving your potted plants a good start with enough water and nutrition, as well as protection from pests, strong winds, and fluctuating temperatures.

Hostas, ferns, and Rodgers' bronze-leaf (opposite) like it wet, to be in partial shade, and with nutrient-rich soil, as these are the conditions in the forests of their native habitats.

Like People, Like Plants

All in all, it really is quite straightforward: plants are living organisms and have many of the same basic needs as us humans. Like plants, we humans need water to avoid dehydration and nutrients to grow and stay healthy. Plants need protection from the cold and the heat, so they don't freeze to death or overheat. When the wind is at its worst or the rain is pouring down, it's wise to whip out an umbrella or find somewhere to seek shelter, in a nook or under a roof. If the plant is lonely and left to fend for itself, it is, of course, difficult to survive on its own. Like people, like plants.

Think of Your Plants as Pals

Treat your plants as you would a friend. A plant is a living thing and needs nurturing, just like a friendship does. A friendship needs time too, and sometimes a little extra attention. If your friend is sick, you should give them a little extra pampering. If the sun is shining, you should offer your friend plenty of water. If your friend overheats, you could offer them shade. If they're looking a little pale, you may suggest they spend an hour in the sun. If they appear malnourished and lethargic, you should get them some nutritious food, and if they hurt themselves, you should offer a helping hand and a pat on the back.

Think of plants as friends who bring you joy and positivity, and reciprocate this by treating them well in return. You know you've got a real case of potted plant fever when you start to anticipate what the plants need and make sure all their needs are met.

Irrigation—What Is the Best Way to Water My Plants?

"How much/often should I water my plants?" This is the question I get asked the most. Watering is an art, yes, but it can also be done easily. I'll explain how here.

"Does your potted plant like a lot of water and consistent moisture?" This is an important question. Some plants love moisture and water, while others dislike too much of it. One piece of knowledge I've gained in my time is that plants that grow quickly and have large leaves and larger flowers, such as the hydrangea, dahlia, and begonia, want and need a lot of water. Naturally, more water is required to produce and transport sustenance and nutrients to such magnificent and exuberant plants. These types of flowers also require fertilizer in addition to plenty of water. Read more about fertilizer on pages 75–81.

Plants with thinner stems and more modest flowers tend to be better able to tolerate drought. In this category we find sage, lavender, and catnip. These flowers can dry out a little between each watering and thus require less attention. Perhaps this type of flower is a good choice for those who are a bit forgetful, have little time, or are frequently away.

Irrigation is important when it comes to transporting nutrients from the soil into the stem, foliage, flowers, and fruit. When the plant is watered, it absorbs that water and also the nutrients into the roots, then takes this sustenance further up the stem and out to the foliage and flowers.

Buddy Up with Your Potted Plants!

Think about how your plants live where they originate from. Do you have a Mediterranean plant or a desert plant that is used to strong sun, high summer temperatures, and long periods without rainwater? Or do you have a plant that grows in more shaded, humid, and rainy forested areas? Try to give your potted plants the same approximate conditions as they're used to back home.

CONTAINER FACTS

The most common causes of plant disease and death:

- Too *much* water—heavy, wet soil over time leads to root rot.
- Too *little* water—drought causes the plant's roots to dry out, so not enough water is sent out into the stem and foliage, and the plant withers and dies.
- Too *little* nutrition—this makes the plant pale, weak, and vulnerable to disease.
- Too *much* nutrition—this puts a lot of stress on the plant and can cause discoloration and poor growth.
- Chilly nights or cold winds will often overwhelm and damage the plant, resulting in what is known as *frost damage*.
- Pests such as aphids often eat parts of the plant and suck out all the nutrients.

CONTAINER FACT

Did you know that lavender, sage, and catnip like to be watered *around* the plant? If you only water in the middle of the pot and *on* the plant itself, you risk the plant becoming too moist, which may then lead it to mold and rot.

How to Water

Remember that *all* the soil should be watered so that the roots can thrive throughout the pot. You should therefore distribute the water around the surface of the soil in a circular motion.

Self-watering systems such as *drip irrigation* and so-called *soaker hoses* are a good investment when the time comes and can be used to water both pots and beds. This is a method of watering plants where water drips slowly and evenly into a pot or bed. The irrigation system can also be connected to a timer, so that watering takes place automatically while you're away.

PLANTING EXAMPLE

My catnip gets lots of sun out on the terrace in a breathable terra-cotta pot that dries up quickly, while my hostas are placed up against a wall where there's a bit more shade and are planted in plastic or glazed pots that retain moisture. By doing this, I'm able to team up with my potted plants and the conditions in which they are meant to thrive and grow, so they don't get homesick. Happy plant = happy gardener.

Catnip is a good choice if you want a hardy potted plant that requires minimal attention, watering, and nutrients. It does well in both pots and boxes and can endure the winter year after year. The only thing it doesn't like is heavy, wet soil over long periods of time.

Maidenhair vine (*Muehlenbeckia complexa*) loves moisture. Typical signs of not getting enough water are brown, dry leaves that shed. Shiny green leaves are a sign of health and tell me that the plant has enough water and nutrients.

CONTAINER TIP

Cut the lawn recently? Take a couple of handfuls of the freshly mown grass and sprinkle it evenly over the potting soil. If you're forecasted a lot of sun and there's a risk of the soil drying up, the grass cuttings help retain moisture and provide the plant with nourishment too.

TEST IF YOUR PLANT NEEDS WATER

The vision test: If you're wondering whether your potted plants need more water, you can do a vision test. If you see the foliage shrinking and the plant looks a bit limp due to lack of water pressure in the stem and leaves, these are signs that it's time to water. Plants are a bit like us humans when we get dehydrated. Our skin wrinkles and we get lethargic. You should preferably avoid letting your plants get that far, but if you do observe this, you'll at least be able to tell that there isn't enough water in the soil, roots, and foliage.

The fingertip test: If the soil feels dry when you touch it, this is also a sign of a lack of water. The soil may even contract so that there is a gap between the edge of the pot and the soil itself. Not sure whether you should water your plant? Use the tip of your finger and push it an inch or so into the soil. Does it feel dry? Then the plant needs watering.

Lift it up: Still in doubt? Lift the pot. A light pot usually means there's not much water in the soil; a heavy pot means there's a lot of water in the soil. Water when the pot feels light, and don't if the pot feels heavy.

Hydrangeas (see page 162) prefer a lot of moisture and watering, as well as being in partial or full shade. This photo was taken when we had a long warm period in the early summer with temperatures reaching over 86°F/30°C, scorching sun, and no rain, which caused the soil to dry up quickly. Hence us getting the umbrella out for some sun protection. Hydrangeas can often curl up if it gets too hot. Fortunately, this plant thrived well into the summer, when the temperature eventually dropped. Place your hydrangea in a spot where it can get some shade during the day.

CONTAINER TIPS

Away on Vacation or Dry Weather in the Forecast?

Here are a few tips for keeping your plants hydrated:

- Cover the potting soil with a thin layer of leaves, freshly cut grass, moss, hedge clippings, or hay. This reduces evaporation, meaning you can water less often.
- Water thoroughly when you first water the plant. This means watering the plant so that water trickles out from the drainage holes below. This only really needs to be done about one or two times a week, depending on the sun and temperature.
- Put your potted plants somewhere with more shade—the plant will drink less and the soil will dry out more slowly.
- Drip irrigation or soaker hoses provide good moisture evenly and use a fraction of the water you need for normal watering cans. Such a system usually only needs to be connected to a tap. Drip irrigation is an investment, but it pays off in the long run, as fewer plants die as a result of overwatering or insufficient watering.

I have a few trusted friends who look after our plants while we're on tour. They often live at our place and look after the plants if we're away for a long time. Control freak? Me?!

CONTAINER TIPS

- Use a nozzle on the garden hose, so that the stream is consistent and gentle. The nozzle makes the stream a lot lighter on the foliage and roots. It's not that different from our skin—it feels much better to have a soft rain shower than a hard, pointed jet of water.
- Use a drip irrigation hose for pots. These are also available with a solar panel, so you won't be dependent on a power connection.
- Collect rainwater in buckets or other containers, ideally under gutters. Rainwater is oxygen-rich, natural, and the best thing for your potted plants.

If you're heading on vacation, you can help ensure that your plants don't dry out:

- Give each plant plenty of water before you leave, but don't soak the soil too much so that it becomes soggy, as the plant may "drown," get root rot, and turn yellow. Try to make the soil evenly moist by giving it a little more water than you would normally.
- Place the pots out of direct sunlight or in a more shaded corner. This means they'll drink less water and won't dry out as fast. If you live in a place prone to rainfall, drying out is rarely a problem.
- Fill a 1½-quart or -liter bottle with water and stick it upside down in the soil at the outer edge of the pot, so that the bottle slowly empties into the soil and the watering is portioned out.
- Place the pots in a large bucket or basin with newspaper or another absorbent material in the bottom. Fill the container with water so that the absorbent material takes in the water. When the plants are placed on the soft material, the roots will absorb the moisture over time, and the soil stays evenly moist.

Principles of Irrigation

Most of us prefer the right temperature water when we bathe or shower. The same applies to plants. You should generally use lukewarm water, as the plant's roots can be overwhelmed by very low or high temperatures.

"I don't like being showered with a power washer, and neither do my plants."

Is it raining out, so you can't do any gardening? How about giving the houseplants a shower in the summer rain for an hour? This natural rinse removes dust and stimulates growth and well-being, and the plants will even grow better afterwards!

Don't use too hard a stream when watering either, as this can damage the foliage and the uppermost roots.

My Best Vacation Watering Tip

Get a good plant friend, or team up with a kind neighbor who doesn't mind dropping by and watering your plants while you're away. It's best if you have a neighbor who also has their own potted plants, so you can be sure that the plants will receive the best possible care while you're away.

CONTAINER TIP

If you're looking to keep some hardy summer flowers outdoors, it's a good idea to think about getting ones that can withstand a drought while you're away, such as geraniums, salvias, or daisies.

Soil

Soil is the brown gold that magically gives life to your plants. The earth is the very foundation of life for both people and plants, so we should treat it with respect, understanding, and love.

To put it simply, good soil produces lush, beautiful potted plants. So what's the best way to get nutrient-rich soil in which the plants can grow and thrive? Good potting soil can, of course, be bought at a garden center, and you can't go far wrong with good potting soil. You can also improve the quality of your soil easily by creating a compost pile with food scraps from your own kitchen, other plant cuttings from your garden, and/or livestock manure, or with ready-made fertilizer mixes.

Potting soil works well for most of your garden plants, except those that like a more acidic soil, such as hydrangeas and rhododendrons. These two should therefore be planted in what is known as ericaceous compost or a soil mix especially formulated for acid-loving plants.

Acidic soil has a low pH, while basic (or alkaline) soil has a high pH. Normally, the pH value in soil is between 4.5 and 5.5 (on a scale that goes from 1 to 14). The vast majority of garden plants do not like acidic soil, but prefer a pH value between 5.5 and 6.5.

CONTAINER TIP

Do you buy potting soil? I try to avoid peat and buy peat-free compost, as it's best for the environment. Draining nature of its peat bogs so that we can buy soil to put in our gardens is destructive and unsustainable.

You can go far with a good potting soil, but you can also add extra nutrients to the soil that the plants will love, such as composted cow manure, chicken manure pellets, or artificial fertilizer/calcium nitrate.

Why Do We Need to Add Nutrients to Soil?

Soil itself is made up of mineral-rich matter that doesn't have nutrients added in. Good soil therefore contains a lot of organic matter with nutrients that the plants need, whether the soil is in your garden, in a field, in the forest, or in a pot. This is particularly important when it comes to container plants as plants in pots will eat up all the nutrients found in the soil over time, at which point we have to add new plant nutrients—compost food scraps, bokashi compost, or artificial fertilizer. And as you can see, there are many products you can use to add nutrients to the soil; choose the one that suits you and your container garden.

Fertilizer and Nutrient Supplements

Over time, your plants will eat up all the nutrients in the soil. For that reason, we have to add new nutrients in the form of fresh soil or fertilizer supplements. If you buy new nutrient-rich potting

Here, my hosta is about to be repotted in a larger pot for the season. I reused some of last year's soil, but added a healthy top layer of fresh soil for good growth, and dug into last year's soil a little to make it lighter and less compact.

soil every year, the plants will generally have all the sustenance they need for the season. But if you've got container garden fever like me, and favor big plants with huge flowers, you can add extra nutrition in the form of fertilizer to ensure your plants reach their maximum potential beyond the summer season.

How can you tell if your plants need some extra nutrition? Many potted plants will, in addition to growing poorly, not develop flowers, and the foliage will often appear pale in color. These are typical signs of a nutrient deficiency, which will mean that the plants are more vulnerable to disease and pests.

You can reuse the soil in large pots for several years. Poke a little at the old soil with a stick and dig a little further in with a spade. Then add new nutrient-rich soil on top before placing your plant back inside.

CONTAINER TIP

Remember that the better the growing conditions for the plants—getting lots of sunlight, are at a comfortable temperature, and receive plenty of water—the more nutrients the plants eat and need. Top up your potted plants with fresh nutrient-rich soil over the existing potting soil, or give them extra plant food a couple of times a month. You can, for example, use fertilizer spikes that you lodge into the soil or liquid plant food that you mix into the water in your watering can.

How to Provide Nutrition

- Add a new top layer of nutrient-rich soil, such as composted cow manure, during the growing season—from May to September.
- If necessary, replace all of the soil if you choose to repot your plant, and use new nutrient-rich soil.
- Add liquid organic homemade plant food consisting of nettle water, herbal distillate, or liquid gold (see pages 80–81).
- Provide artificial plant nutrients, either in liquid form mixed into water or by sprinkling slow-release pellets on top, which gradually dissolve and sink into the soil as the plant is watered.

Used organic tea bags can be pushed into the potting soil. They add nutrition and even retain water! It's a great tip for if you're going on vacation and are worried about your potted plants drying out.

Collect eggshells in a container, crush them, and mix it into or sprinkle it on top of the plant soil. Eggshells contain lots of calcium, which plants like tomatoes need and love.

CONTAINER TIP

Other Useful Nutritional Advice

Coffee is rich in nitrogen and serves as good plant nutrition. Do you have a splash of coffee left in your cup or carafe? Mix it with water and pour it over the potting soil. The mixture should contain one part coffee to five parts water.

Eggshells are nutritious and add calcium to the soil. Save your eggshells over the winter and add them to the potting soil a couple of times throughout the season. It's a good idea to mix a little into the potting soil too.

Liquid plant food is a good nutritional supplement. Use a couple of times a month during the growing season. You can make it yourself or buy it.

Liquid Plant Food

Available in most home centers and plant nurseries in organic and artificial formulations, liquid plant food is added to the water you use to water your plants. The mixing ratio is often one part plant food to ten parts water, but always check the instructions first, as it is powerful and concentrated stuff. If the plants get too much nutrition, they are overwhelmed and can become sick and unhappy.

Plant Food You Can Make Yourself

Nettle Water

Grab a large plastic bucket—I use a mason tub—and fill it with nettles (preferably fresh new shoots). Pour water into the bucket right up to the brim and put it somewhere sunny for a few weeks. Then, remove the nettles, and you have the world's best nitrogen-rich fertilizer for your plants. Cheap and sustainable. I use around one part nettle water to ten parts water that I then water the potting soil with. I do this one to three times a month during the growing season from May to September, depending on the plant's nutritional needs. Nettle water has a horrible smell, though, so place the bucket a good distance from the house or any seating area. Fortunately, the smell disappears when the nettle water is absorbed into the soil.

For acid-loving plants like hydrangeas and rhododendrons, you can add a handful of forest soil, pine needle cuttings, coffee grounds, or a splash of coffee to the soil to increase the acidity.

CONTAINER TIP

Annual summer flowers can benefit from a nitrogen-rich fertilizer from August to September, for example calcium nitrate, so that you get the full potential out of the plant throughout the fall. Perennial plants will eventually go dormant for the winter, so I don't want to stimulate more growth, but rather help the plant wind down. For these types of plants, I don't give any fertilizer from September onward.

Liquid Gold

Mix one part urine to ten parts water, which you will then distribute over the plant soil. Some blanch at the thought, but come on, folks—urine is one of the cleanest substances on the planet, and we all want healthy potted plants. In the past, this was a common method of adding nutrients to the garden. Fortunately, the focus and awareness of natural healthy plant food is increasing again, looking back to methods that have existed all along. Get yourself a bucket and pee in it throughout the summer, and you'll have an excellent nitrogen-rich source of plant food for your tomatoes and other plants in your outdoor space.

Calcium Nitrate

Calcium nitrate is a nitrogen-rich artificial fertilizer, and I like to mix a small handful of calcium nitrate balls into a 2½-gallon/10-liter jug of water. Always mix according to the instructions for use. Some flowers need a lot of nitrogen-rich nutrition, such as angel's trumpets (*Brugmansia* spp.) (see pages 88–89).

CONTAINER FACT

We often say that we feed the plant, but in reality we're actually feeding the soil. When you water the plant, its roots drink up and absorb the water from the soil. Through this, the nutrients are carried up into the plant and out into the stem, foliage, and flowers.

Coleus cuttings on the windowsill in May became beautiful outdoor potted plants in July. Coleus likes to be somewhere sunny and warm outdoors or in a greenhouse. The cutting can be placed in water for root development and then planted in soil. They can also be stuck straight into moist soil for propagation.

CONTAINER FACT

The best time for propagation is in the spring and summer months. The plants can then grow and thrive and are ripe and ready for the growing season—a perfect time to make new baby plants.

Plant Propagation

When the spring sun returns in March and April, you can start propagating cuttings indoors. These plants will come to life and be ready for a new growing season. This is the perfect time for plant propagation, because the plants are full of energy and ready to grow and reproduce. You can buy plants, but in my experience, I always feel best when producing my own plants from a mother plant—that is, a main plant from which you can take a cutting or offshoot.

Propagating from Cuttings

There are various methods of propagating your plant collection, either starting from seed or propagating cuttings and offshoots. Here you can see an example of cutting propagation.

The fig is a particularly amenable and fast-growing cutting plant. Find a friend with a small fig tree and ask for a cutting. See more on page 255.

CONTAINER FACT

Container plants that are easy to propagate from cuttings:

- Coleus (*Coleus* spp.)
- Geranium (*Pelargonium* spp.)
- Angel's trumpets (*Brugmansia* spp.) (see pages 88–89)
- Fig (*Ficus carica*) (see page 252)
- Vervain (*Verbena* spp.) (see pages 176–181)
- Tomatoes (see pages 222–226)
- Papyrus (*Cyperus papyrus*) (see pages 172–175)

Top cuttings of coleus in water. Place the cutting in sun, for example, in the kitchen window. Change the water a couple of times a month, and you'll be rewarded with lovely cuttings and healthy roots. After a couple of weeks to a couple of months, you'll see delicate roots forming—a good sign that your plant is ready to be transplanted into potting soil.

How to Propagate Coleus Cuttings

- Cut the top of the coleus's branches, about 4 to 6 inches/ 10 to 15 cm.
- Remove the lowest leaves.
- Place the cutting in a clear glass/bottle with water.
- Place the cutting on a sunny windowsill.
- Change the water once a week.
- After about one to six weeks, the cutting will develop roots.
- Plant the cutting in soil (see page 87).

CONTAINER TIP

You can put the fresh coleus cutting straight into wet potting soil (without having had it in water) in spring or summer. If there is sufficient light and a stable temperature, it does not need to have developed its roots in water before it is transplanted into the soil. As long as there are good growing conditions, the cutting will quickly develop roots and grow in the new potting soil.

Taking stem cuttings is easy. Some plants are easier than others, such as the hugely popular coleus. With good care, coleus can grow large, and they can thrive both as indoor and outdoor plants in the summer months.

Cuttings in glass bottles, jam jars, or small vases are both practical and look beautiful on your windowsill.

CONTAINER TIP

Coleus often produces flowers, but I recommend plucking them off, as they drain the plant of a lot of nutrients and make the color of the leaves weaker. In any case, I think the leaves of this plant are its most exciting feature.

CONTAINER TIP

In May through August, the sprouting and growing conditions are often so good that you can place the cutting directly into moist soil, where it will eventually take root.

How to Plant Cuttings in Soil

- Fill a pot with soil—I recommend one with holes in the base.
- Water the soil thoroughly.
- Stick your finger into the soil and make a hole in the middle.
- Insert the cutting into the hole, so deep that all the roots are covered.
- Pack/squeeze the soil carefully around the cutting.
- Remember to keep the soil moist, so that the roots can establish themselves in the pot.
- Put the transplanted cuttings somewhere warm and bright, for example, on a windowsill, or in a sunny corner or greenhouse.

Hostas are best divided in late fall or early spring. Loosen and pull the entire root ball out of the pot, place the spade in the middle, and split it in half. Then place one half back in the pot, the other half in a new pot and fill with soil. And just like that you've got two hostas, isn't that great? Homegrown and affordable. Perfect for those of us with a case of container garden fever!

Division Propagation

Some plants can be propagated by division. You can do this by dividing an existing plant root into several parts and getting two to four plants from one. This is a smart way to make more.

Father and son. Angel's trumpets (*Brugmansia* spp.,left and opposite) are great to get cuttings from. Cut a branch and put it in moist soil in spring and summer, or leave it in water for a couple of weeks for the roots to develop. The cutting often shrivels up a bit in the first few days, but then the stem in the soil will take in water, the roots will start to grow, and the plant brightens up again.

How big can you grow your angel's trumpets? They can grow as big as trees, like here in Portugal, where we like to vacation. They can reach an incredible size even in a pot, often growing 3 to 6 feet/1 to 2 meters high and wide (see the angel's trumpets in chapter 3, pages 88–89).

This agapanthus (*Agapanthus* spp., left) is as tall as me at 6 feet/2 meters. My agapanthus is smaller than this, but a hardy, pretty little plant that can be nicely split in two for propagation in fall or spring. Agapanthus is also one of the few plants that likes its roots to be tightly packed in—in fact, it prefers them a little cramped, hence the sheer amount of roots in this pot.

Seed Propagation

Some seeds are tiny, like poppy seeds, others are slightly larger, such as sunflower seeds, and others are really rather large, like avocado seeds (yes, the avocado pit is a seed). You can think of a seed as an embryo of life protected by a shell. Beautiful, isn't it?

In this "embryo," there is a lot of energy waiting to be released. The seed needs moisture from water and warmer temperatures to start the germination process and, as it grows, it also needs plenty of sunlight and nutrients from the soil. For that reason, you should sow in spring, when the days become longer, the sunlight stronger, and the temperature higher.

And yes, I am fascinated every single time by how a few hard sunflower seeds can turn into sunflowers over 6 feet/2 meters tall in my pots (see project 7 on sunflowers, pages 187–191).

You can also sow the seeds, cover them with a sheet of plastic, and place them on a warm floor to germinate within a week. Remove the plastic when the seeds sprout. A good tip is to mark the seeds with labels, so you remember what was sown and where.

Grow Lights and Heat Mats

Many of us with potted plants are impatient and long for spring, and therefore start sowing seeds indoors in small pots as early as January and February. If this is you, grow lights can be of great help. In short, grow lights give the plants an artificial light spectrum that resembles natural sunlight to a much greater extent than ordinary light bulbs.

Grow lights have become readily available and are often found at garden centers or online, and some of these bulbs can be screwed into regular lamp sockets too. There are people who also use a heat mat under their pots to increase the temperature for good germination.

CONTAINER FACT

A normal incandescent bulb has around 2700 Kelvin. LED light bulbs measure in at somewhat more, while plants like between 3000 and 6000 Kelvin—which grow lights can offer. In other words, if you're in the market for a grow light, check the amount of Kelvin it has before you buy. I only use white grow lights, as they are versatile and work for most of us.

A small cultivation garden with grow lights placed under the dining table in February, with chiles, bell peppers, and tomatoes (see pages 222–226) that we sowed from seed. You can also sow vervain (see pages 176–181), geranium (see page 156), and purple bell vine (*Rhodochiton atrosanguineum*) seeds.

"Taking care of flowers and plants in the container garden gives me a sense of peace and relaxation from a sometimes hectic everyday life. The sight of plants growing and thriving, flowers sprouting, and tomatoes ripening makes me happy and encourages me to continue feeding my creativity."

From March through April, the days get longer, the temperature rises, and you can now place your young plants near a sunny window. When the danger of frost is over, these can be transplanted outside into larger pots. By sowing seeds inside, you give the potted plants a head start, and you can enjoy their flowers, berries, and fruit earlier and for longer throughout the growing season.

Opposite: An avocado tree cultivated from an avocado pit.

CONTAINER FACT

Did you know that avocados, mangos, and citrus fruit have seeds you can grow on a kitchen windowsill into small exotic trees?

Tubers vs. Bulbs

A **tuber** is a swollen underground stem that has everything it needs to take root, sprout, and grow. As the tuber shoots up, it gradually turns into a magnificent flower. Most tubers in my potted garden have to be dug up and kept inside—where they're frost-free—throughout the winter.

A **bulb** is characterized by the fact that it has several layers. Inside the bulb is everything needed to create a colorful tulip or daffodil. In the bulb there is a germ waiting to sprout. Most bulbs, like tulips, are put in the ground in fall, and they are among the first to sprout up through the soil in the spring. Many bulbs can therefore withstand staying in the ground through the winter.

I think flowering bulbs are spring's most beautiful sensation in my container garden. When the spring sun takes hold, the bulbs we planted the previous fall come to life and burst into colorful blooms, much to the delight of those of us with container garden fever.

Tulips and daffodils are good bulbous plants for those of you fond of early spring flowers in your pots.

My favorite tuberous plants (opposite, bottom) are: gladioli (which grow from corms); wood sorrels (*Oxalis* spp., which grow from rhizomes); and begonias and dahlias. It's hard to believe that a small tuber (below) can turn into a massive 5-foot/1.5-meter-tall dahlia, with flowers the size of dinner plates (left, top)! It's just incredible—no wonder I've got container garden fever!

CHAPTER 3 SUMMARY

Caring for Your Potted Plants

- Remember that your container garden is a great place to switch off and relax throughout all four seasons.
- Watering your plants can be easier than you think: remember the vision, fingertip, and lifting tests, and you're sure to crack the watering code.
- I encourage the use of peat-free soil with added nutrients, and there's a lot of those we can use here: eggshells, coffee, composted cow manure, or homemade plant food.
- Propagating plants is a simple method of creating a container garden on a tight budget, and the easiest way to succeed is with cuttings and division propagation.
- Remember that people and plants have many similarities, including when it comes to well-being and care.

CHAPTER 4

PEST CONTROL

CONTAINER TIP

Remember to check your plants (including the potting soil) when you buy them, both for pests and snails—you don't want to bring them into your garden.

What Exactly Are Pests?

Have you ever had lice? Then you know how unpleasant and uncomfortable they are. Plants can also get lice (known as aphids), and they'll appreciate you even more if you can help get rid of them. Fortunately, there's lots of good advice out there on how to do so!

The biggest nightmare for those of us involved with container gardening—and it is the same for every gardening enthusiast—is to find that our beautiful plants are being attacked by pests. You will notice that the plant is growing poorly, that its leaves have turned yellow, sticky, and may even have curled, or that the leaves have a gray-white coating. Other times you can see that caterpillars have eaten the foliage. You will usually see the pests if you inspect the leaves closely, especially underneath.

How to Detect Pests

Where you'll find the pest varies, but I've generally found that checking the underside of the foliage helps. You will often find aphids there, which look like tiny creepy-crawlies.

CONTAINER FACT

The term "pest" is somewhat misleading, because most often the culprits are just ordinary insects and snails. But if there are too many of them, they will still destroy your potted plants. The most common types are:

- Aphids
- Whiteflies
- Spider mites
- Thrips
- Snails and slugs

What these pests have in common is that they either eat the foliage or suck the nutrients out of the plants. The plants often get sick and in the worst case die.

Ladybugs are both beautiful and useful to us plant lovers. They eat aphids. We would, of course, like as many ladybugs and other beneficial organisms among our potted plants as possible.

Beneficial Bugs

There are also animals that are good for our potted plants. These are called beneficial organisms and are small insects that we *want* in our outdoor space. Beneficial organisms often eat up the pests and are therefore good friends to those of us with container garden fever.

Typical beneficial organisms include:

- Ladybugs
- Spiders
- Parasitoid wasps
- Green lacewings

These animals gobble up the pests and help keep the pest population down. Nature's very own pest control!

How to Get Rid of Pests

You can prevent infestation by taking care of your plants so that they stay healthy and fresh. Should something go wrong and you do find pests, remember to breathe deeply and remind yourself that there is plenty of good advice out there to overcome the problem. Pest control can be done in various ways. Here are my best methods:

> **"Finding that your plants have aphids and other pests is something that all of us have experienced from time to time. In my experience, prevention measures work best."**

Cold Water

You can go a long way with a cold jet of water. Spray water (to the extent that the plant can tolerate it) using a steady stream on the foliage and stem. Feel free to massage the pests away with your fingers, and cut away the parts of the plant that have taken the most damage. Repeat the rinsing process again after a week.

CONTAINER FACT

Did you know that if you have lots of flowering potted plants, the flowers attract beneficial organisms, and it will be easier for you to keep pests away? Sowing a selection of meadow flowers in a flower box (see pages 182–185) could be a good idea and a natural way to keep pests from making their way into your container garden.

Green Soap Water

Recipe for Green Soap Water

Add one part liquid green soap (see caption, opposite) to ten parts lukewarm water. In addition to working as a pest control, the plants will often take on a glistening shimmer when showered with green soap water. You should avoid spraying them with this mixture when it is particularly sunny out, as you may risk the plants getting sun damage. Think of it like how you shouldn't smear yourself with Vaseline or baby oil and then lie in the sun.

You can also use natural hand sanitizer on the leaves and stems of any plants suffering from pest damage. Smear some hand sanitizer on the foliage and stem, and massage it into both sides of the leaves. Repeat after a week if necessary.

Planting in pots can also give you better control over pests like brown slugs. If you discover slugs in your garden, try wrapping copper foil tape around the bottom part of the pot or around the entirety of your container garden. Slugs and snails do not like copper.

CONTAINER TIP

Alternatives to green soap water include nettle water (see page 80) and bokashi water (a liquid byproduct of bokashi compost—but you can use any kind of compost tea), which is sprayed directly onto the plants. Both of these options work well as pest control.

Green soap is a vegetable oil–based, water-soluble, environmentally safe soap often used by tattoo artists to promote healing. When I get new plants, I always check them over first, and then spray the plants with green soap water, both above and below the foliage, as well as on the stem. The green soap forms a protective film around the plant, which means that aphids and larvae avoid the plant or get stuck and die in the sticky soap-water mixture. Green soap is a good preventive measure to deter pests. If you do discover pests, you can increase the amount of green soap you add to the water mixture.

CONTAINER TIP

If necessary, you can add a touch of rubbing alcohol to the green soap mixture. Then the aphids, which cannot tolerate these chemicals, should die. You should limit or avoid the use of chemical agents, though, as those unfortunately kill a number of beneficial organisms that we *want* in our potted plants.

Cut away any visible damaged branches and the most infested parts of the plant.

CHAPTER 4 SUMMARY

Pest Control

- Common pests, such as aphids, spider mites, thrips, whiteflies, and slugs and snails, can threaten your plants' well-being. These pests eat foliage or suck the nutrients out of the plants.
- Ladybugs, parasitic wasps, and spiders are examples of beneficial organisms that eat the above-mentioned pests, and are therefore good for your potted plants. Think of them as nature's very own pest control.
- Discoloration, poor growth, shiny streaks on the foliage, and sticky droppings indicate a pest infestation. The underside of the foliage or at the top of the newest shoots is often where you'll find plant lice.
- Cold water spray, green soap water, and hand sanitizer are good ways to fight pests. Wrapping copper foil tape around a pot is an environmentally friendly way to keep slugs away. Chemical agents should be limited to protect the other beneficial organisms and nature.
- Sowing meadow flowers in a planter can attract beneficial animals and help keep pests away.

CHAPTER 5

WINTER

Wintering Outdoors

When I say *winter plants,* I mean container plants that are able to survive the entire winter outdoors. These are referred to as perennials.

Ten Perennials That Can Withstand Winter Outdoors

Make sure to check with your local nursery about what varieties are cold-hardy in your microclimate, as some ferns and grasses, for example, have tropical varieties.

- Hosta
- Clematis
- Cold-hardy ferns like *Dryopteris filix-mas* and *Matteuccia struthiopteris*
- Cold-hardy ornamental grasses like *Calamagrostis* ×*acutiflora* 'Karl Foerster', *Helictotrichon sempervirens*, and *Panicum virgatum*
- Catnip (*Nepeta cataria*)
- Coral bells (*Heuchera sanguinea*)
- Lavender (*Lavandula* spp.)
- Sage (hardy varieties of *Salvia* spp.)
- Bleeding heart (*Lamprocapnos spectabilis*, syn. Dicentra spectabilis)
- Garden scabious (*Scabiosa caucasica*)

Read more about perennials and evergreens in the section on hardiness zones on pages 36–38.

CONTAINER TIP

How to Help Your Potted Plants Survive Outdoors

- Place them against a wall or under a roof, so that they're as snug as possible. It is often the subzero winter winds that result in plants freezing to death.
- Huddle the containers together and cover them with leaves or burlap sacks. These work like a protective winter blanket.

Olive trees can withstand a couple of frosty nights but should be kept indoors over the winter.

Wintering Indoors

Many plants will survive the winter indoors until spring if you bring them in before the frost arrives. They should be put back outside again when the risk of frost has passed; check your USDA zone map for the average last frost date in your area.

Indoor Wintering Guide

There are a few basic principles that apply to all potted plants, covering temperature, light, watering, and nutrition.

Temperature

- Around 40° to 50°F/5° to 10°C (depending on the plant variety) is ideal.
- Avoid major temperature fluctuations.

Geraniums are one of the most widespread and popular summer flowers. They can winter well inside and then be put back out in the spring. We keep many of our geraniums in a cool bedroom throughout the winter, or downstairs in the frost-free basement.

Light

- Plants need access to some light, either from a window or a grow light.
- The lower the temperature, the less light the plant needs.
- The higher the temperature, the more light the plant needs.

Water

- Keep the soil on the dry side—it should only be slightly moist.
- If the plants are kept somewhere cool, they'll only want and need a little water.
- Water little and often. Wet soil over time causes root rot and other diseases.

Nutrition

- No fertilizer is needed during the dormancy period, but if you use grow lights, you can give them a small maintenance dose of plant food, especially in February when they start to come to life again. If the leaves look pale and the green color disappears, this is a sign that they need some nutrition.

CONTAINER FACTS

Mediterranean Plants That Can Winter Indoors

- Citrus
- Palms
- Olive (*Olea europaea*)
- Fig (*Ficus carica*)
- Kiwi (*Actinidia* spp.)
- Common myrtle (*Myrtus communis*)

Summer Flowers That Can Winter Indoors

- Angel's trumpet (*Brugmansia* spp.)
- Geranium (*Pelargonium* spp.)
- Purple bell vine (*Rhodochiton atrosanguineum*)
- Fuchsia (*Fuchsia* spp.)
- Passionflower (*Passiflora* spp.)
- Heliotrope (*Heliotropium arborescens*)
- Sage (*Salvia* spp.)
- Climbing snapdragon (*Maurandya scandens*, syn. *Asarina scandens*)
- Marguerite daisy (*Argyranthemum* spp.)

Tuberous/Bulbous Plants That Can Winter Indoors

- False shamrock (*Oxalis triangularis*) (a rhizome)
- Dahlia
- Tuberous begonia
- Gladiolus (grows from a corm)

When I lived in Oslo, I kept my olive tree and citrus plants in a cool unheated staircase next to a window. Perfect conditions for wintering.

CONTAINER FACT

Plant varieties have somewhat different needs for light during the winter. In my experience, deciduous plants and shrubs (such as figs and kiwi) do well in darker conditions (without grow lights), while my citrus plants and summer flowers prefer good access to light, either from a window or from grow lights.

Where Can I Winter My Plants?

Do you have access to a basement, storage room, outbuilding, or garage? The principle here is that wintering works best when the plants are kept somewhere bright and cool. Perhaps you have a bedroom on the cooler side that could be suitable for wintering? You're most likely to succeed with keeping your potted plants alive and well at a temperature of around 40°F/5°C, but you *can* also succeed in temperatures from 35° to 50°F/1° to 15°C, depending on the plant variety.

It *is* possible to keep your plants alive and well in your living room over the winter, but most plants won't do as well as they would outdoors and will lose lots of their foliage because, for most of us, the air in our homes is too dry, the temperature too high, and they simply do not get enough sunlight throughout the winter months.

The main challenge you might find here is the fact that it needs to be cool and bright for the plant, which is rarely the case in rooms we live in. Many people have tried to keep olive trees in the living room, only to see the leaves fall off and scatter all over the floor.

Grow Lights or Sunlight from the Window?

I use both. I have a room in the basement that gets natural light from a window, and I also have a room in the basement without a window, in which I use grow lights. It is generally easier to succeed with grow lights, as the plants have a guaranteed, consistent light source.

Plants want about twelve to sixteen hours of light a day and—just like us—prefer it dark at night. I use a timer on my grow lights so they automatically turn the lights on and off.

Grow lights in the basement

CONTAINER TIP

Tuberous plants like wood sorrel, dahlias, and begonias have tubers underground that you can dig up and keep dry, dark, and cool in a box lined with newspaper.

Step 1: Check the weather forecast.

When the first report of a night frost and freezing temperatures is announced, I bring the plants inside. It isn't always the cold temperatures that take the plants first, but rather the cold wind, as this is often even harder on the plants, as well as the combination of the two.

Step 2: Rinse the plant with cold water.

Before bringing the plants indoors, I rinse the leaves and branches with cold water, such as from a garden hose—but within reason, so the leaves and branches don't break. This way, the plant is cleaned, and you can flush away any pests and aphids.

Step 3: Give it a cut and trim.

If the plant has any broken branches or withered leaves, I cut these off. You don't have to prune and cut back the growth, but it will reduce the size of the plant. This then saves space, and you also reduce the risk of bringing any pests and aphids inside. Pruning is often a growth stimulant for plants anyway, and makes the flowers even more lush in the spring.

Step 4: Give the plants a shower with green soap water.

I also give the plants a good shower with green soap water (see the recipe for this on page 112) before setting them aside for the winter. This treatment cleans the plant, and the green soap mixture forms a protective layer against disease and pests throughout the season.

Step 5: Keep an eye on your plants through the winter.

Check on the plants a couple of times a month throughout the winter. Keep an eye on whether they need a little more water and moisture. Remember that the soil should be slightly moist, but not wet. Feel free to give the potted plants an extra shower with green soap water during the winter to protect them from pests and aphids.

Woo-hoo! The ivy in the balcony box survived the winter resting period in the basement and is ready for a new season. The geranium too! It is pale, malnourished, and ready for some plant food.

What to Do in the Spring Before the Plants Go Back Outside

You can increase the amount of water you give them in February when the days are longer, the temperature rises, and the plants come to life. Gradually increase the amount of water until the plants are ready to be put outside. The pots can be put out again when the risk of frost is over. For most of us, that means sometime in April or May.

Plant Makeover

Keeping your plants alive over the winter is easier than many people think, and anyone can do it. For me and my container plants, there's a lot of love in this period too, and I look forward to taking care of them in the darker months. I personally feel that the transition from winter to spring is a magical time, when nature wakes up again. That's when I know that a new growing season is just around the corner, and my pots and planters will once again be overflowing with flowers, foliage, and fruit.

CONTAINER TIP

Give the plants a makeover before placing them outside. Cut away any dead branches and leaves, and, ideally, you should also change the soil. The plants need and want more nutrient-rich soil once the growing season starts up again.

Remember: when the plant is ready to be put back outside, the key is a gradual transition. Placing them somewhere with plenty of shade, or putting them back out during a period of cloudy weather is good for the first few weeks, or cover them with fiber cloth, a fleece blanket, sheet, or straw for this period.

CHAPTER 5 SUMMARY

Winter

- Some perennials and evergreens can overwinter outdoors, as they go dormant in the fall and reawaken in spring.
- Examples of container plants that can thrive outdoors include hosta, ferns, catnip, lavender, and bleeding heart.
- Many plant varieties require indoor wintering. Summer flowers and less hardy plants should be brought in before the frost arrives. Many potted plants can thrive indoors through the winter and until next spring.
- For wintering indoors, remember: the temperature should be kept around 40° to 50°F/5° to 10°C, they need moderate light, slightly moist soil, and zero to minimal fertilizer. A grow light or natural light from a window is recommended.
- Gradually increase the amount of water as spring approaches, give the plants a makeover before placing them back outside, and when you do put them back outside, protect them from the sun and cold wind for the first few weeks with some sort of cover.

CHAPTER 6

THE YEAR-ROUND CONTAINER GARDEN

Spring: March to May

With spring comes more sunlight and warmer temperatures—even though it takes time before the frost lets go, the potting season is now in full swing.

- Sow seedlings indoors in a sunny window in March/April. With edible plants, such as chiles, bell peppers, and tomatoes, or ornamental plants such as geraniums, vervain, or purple bell vine, you can start as early as January/February with the help of some grow lights.
- Propagation by cuttings (see page 83) can be done indoors in the February–May period, under either a window or grow lights. The more light and the higher the temperature, the faster your cuttings will grow.
- Potting up (see page 207) tuberous plants, such as dahlias and begonias, can be done indoors from March–May.
- Caring for your potted plants over the winter. They come to life in the spring after the winter resting period. Gradually give them more water and nutrition in line with the spring sun and increasing temperatures outside.
- Clean, brush, and wash last year's pots.
- Prune trees and bushes in pots before the leafing period (see page 203).
- Always water perennial and evergreen potted plants that have wintered outside in the spring, as many plants die from drying out even if they look moist.
- Place your potted plants outdoors once the danger of frost is over, and protect them from the strong spring sun for the first few weeks.
- Buy annual summer flowers or perennials and evergreens, and plant them outside when the risk of frost has passed.
- The earliest edible plants to sprout in your container garden, such as chives, can often be harvested as early as April/May.

Tomat Fuzzy Wuzzy
Tomat Black cherry
Tomat Black cherry
Tomat Black cherry
San Marzano
San Marzano

CONTAINER TIP

If there is a risk of night frost after placing the containers outside, you can keep them inside cardboard boxes during the first week, so it's easier to move them outside during the day and back in at night.

Summer: June to August

The growing season is at its peak in the summer, and your creativity can now bear fruit. Now you can sit back, relax, and enjoy the work you've put in through the spring and early summer.

- You can now safely plant and cultivate your favorite potted plants.
- You can improve the soil quality in larger pots and planters by adding fresh nutrient-rich soil, compost, or composted livestock manure products.
- You can repot potted plants that need more soil and more space.
- You can sow seeds directly into your pots and planters, for example, sunflower or various other flower seeds, as long as it's not too late in summer, otherwise there won't be time for it to flourish and flower before the days get too short.
- Add plant food, especially to the larger potted plants that require more nutrients.
- Pale leaves, little growth, and few flowers are often signs of a nutrient deficiency.
- Prune or remove (deadhead) any withered flowers for better growth and new buds.
- Water even more during particularly sunny or dry periods without rain.
- Harvesting of culinary herbs and other edible plants is done throughout the summer.

Cover your pots and planters with plant waste—this protects the potted plants against the cold and nourishes the soil. In the photo above, you can see gladioli clippings covering my herb boxes.

Fall: September to November

The gardening season is by no means over once fall arrives. This time of year delivers many edible plants from your container garden, as well as a rich abundance of flowers from many late-blooming plants. The growth does now slow down and you can pretty much potter around the garden, relax, and pick flowers for your indoor vases or enjoy a cup of tea made with homegrown mint from your own containers.

- Final harvesting of the potted crops, whether that's herbs, tomatoes, onions, or potatoes.
- Annual flowers can be fed with nitrogen-rich fertilizer for a final blooming boost.
- You should now stop feeding all evergreen and perennial potted plants that will be left outside to enter their dormant period over the winter.
- Take cuttings of propagation-friendly flowers such as geraniums, and store indoors until next spring.

- Put any bulbs such as tulips in potting soil.
- Bring in potted plants that cannot withstand frost, such as Mediterranean plants, and those that you want to keep frost-free indoors over the winter. Spray them with green soap water to prevent an aphid infestation (see more about this in the pest control chapter).
- Take cut flowers and decorate your indoor space with plants that bloom in late summer, such as dahlias.
- Clean up your outdoor space and sprinkle leaves, plant waste, and dead flowers as a cover for your pots.
- Place pots with any plants that can survive the winter outdoors snug against a wall or in a corner, where they'll be less exposed to the wind.
- Place pots that will be left outside over the winter slightly above ground before the frost arrives so they don't freeze onto the ground iself.
- Decorate your front stoop area with potted plants in the fall that can withstand a little frost, such as Christmas rose (*Helleborus niger*), heather, or small evergreen shrubs and trees.

One challenge in getting perennials to survive the winter in pots is that the roots are more exposed to frost than if they were buried in the ground. They can also suffer from drought if it turns out to be a cold spring with lots of sun and wind. You should therefore place them against a warm wall to avoid unexpected frosts, and remember to water the containers in early spring to keep them from drying out—even if they look wet from melting snow.

Winter: December to February

Winter has arrived. This is the time when you can relax and look forward to next year's adventures in your outdoor space. Winter is lovely in its own way and can offer unexpected plant joy, such as seeing your ornamental grasses glisten in the white frost and glorious winter sun. Is there anything more beautiful?

- Now is the time to relax a bit and find inspiration. Read gardening books or watch gardening shows.
- How about getting some houseplants? A few good options include the Swiss cheese plant (*Monstera deliciosa*), golden pothos (*Epipremnum aureum*), wax plant (*Hoya* spp.), and various types of cacti and succulents.
- If you have a garden water mirror, garden hoses, or a fountain in your container garden, make sure they are emptied of water, so they don't burst or crack when the frost comes.
- If you want wildlife such as squirrels and birds to visit your garden, hang up feeders around your container garden.
- How about growing microgreens like edible pea shoots on the windowsill?
- Check your pots a couple of times a month and make sure the soil is slightly moist. In the event of any pest infestations, spray the plants with green soap water or other sustainable pest control mixtures.
- It's a good idea to check your tubers and discard any that have developed soft spots. The tubers that have dried out should be misted with water.
- Consider starting to sow some of next season's seeds indoors as early as January or February. Grow lights will be an advantage here.

On the run up to Christmas, I like to decorate our entrance with frost-hardy potted plants such as Christmas roses (*Helleborus niger*), skimmia, heather, and small evergreen trees and shrubs. I put these in pots on the stairs. Feel free to plant some of them in the same pot too. Or add to the atmosphere with outdoor fairy lights and, if you have a roof over your porch, a sheepskin throw on the back of a chair. If the temperature drops below 25°F/−4°C, I take the plants inside and then put them back out again when it's a bit milder.

COLD (PLANT) FEET?

Keep your potted plants from getting cold feet. Raise them off the ground slightly using wooden blocks, pot feet, styrofoam, or other insulating materials. Move them to a milder corner of your outdoor space so they are protected from the wind, or bring them inside.

CHAPTER 7

CONTAINER GARDEN PROJECTS

You don't need a hundred pots like me—you can easily start with two or a few more. Begin with whatever you like, whatever you find most pleasing, and remember to take color, size, and your budget into account. Perhaps you like edible plants or are you more into ornamental plants, or, like me, love both? In this chapter, you'll find my suggestions and ideas for what to put in your pots and planters. These are ideas that anyone can do and that will reward you with lots of plant joy in the future!

PROJECT 1: SUMMER FLOWERS

Looking for plants that are simple, easy to care for, and yield quick results? Buy yourself annual flowers every spring or summer if you don't want to sow them yourself. I buy a selection every year in the spring, which I plant in pots and planters. That way I ensure early flowering in my outdoor space. And, as long as you give them regular care and a little attention, your annual flowers will last until the frost comes.

What You Will Need

A selection of your favorite annual flowers, a couple of pots, and some potting soil.

Care

- Repot your new flowers into larger pots with fresh soil. The plants are often already too big for the pots they are grown in, and the soil will be lacking in nutrients.
- Feel free to double or triple the size of the new pot.
- Use good nutrient-rich soil, preferably especially formulated for flowering plants, with enough nutrients to last for most of the season.
- Add extra plant food (see pages 75–81) throughout the summer for good growth. Few flowers, poor growth, and pale leaves are signs of a nutrient deficiency.
- Ensure a steady supply of water. Choose varieties that can tolerate less water, so-called drought-resistant plants, if you have less time to spend gardening. The more sun and heat, the more the flowers will drink.

- If you have leftover soil in the pots and planters from last year, you won't need to change all the soil, but you will need to improve it (see pages 75–81).
- Regularly pluck off any dead flowers, as this will provide the plant with more energy, helping it produce new flowers and grow stronger throughout the season.
- Cut back the summer flowers by about one-third after deadheading in midsummer. They will often then bloom again in late summer.
- If the plants become long and thin, so that the stem breaks easily, you can cut them back about halfway down. That way, they will grow larger and have a stronger main stem and growth.

How

See chapter 2 for information on planting and maintenance.

Good to Know

Flowering annuals are gorgeous and beautify your outdoor space, but they also have other important functions. They attract lots of insects, which both prevent pests on your other flowers and even pollinate them, which is important for food production. Our neighbor has bees and produces honey, so our summer flowers are frequented by honey bees, as well as lots of butterflies and bumblebees, just to name a few.

CONTAINER TIP

Planting a variety of flowers together in a larger container creates an exciting and diverse aesthetic. In this pot, I've planted annual cosmos at the back and smaller summer dahlias at the front. They are planted together in a large plastic container with holes in the base and then placed on top of an old oil barrel, to make for a distinctive and unique pot to add to the container garden.

My Favorite Summer Flowers

Pansy (*Viola ×wittrockiana,* opposite, top row): One of the earliest annuals to bloom and a sure sign of spring. Because it can withstand a little frost and endure temperatures a few degrees below freezing, it is one of the safest flowers to plant in pots and balcony boxes in the spring. It is available in a range of colors and sizes, so offers something for everyone with container garden fever. It thrives in ordinary potting soil and likes even moisture. This flower blooms in early summer, but if you pluck off any dead flowers, you'll give the plant energy for another round of flowering during the summer. The pansy is edible and can be used as a decoration for cakes and salads.

Lobelia (*Lobelia* spp., opposite, middle row, right) and **petunia** (*Petunia* spp., opposite, middle row, left and middle): Fancy having hundreds of flowers on one plant? You'll get plenty of blossoms for your buck with lobelia (left) and petunias. For the lobelia, you don't have to deadhead, whereas you should do so regularly with your petunia plant. Trailing lobelia is one of the best summer flowers if you like a hanging basket. Thrives in full sun to partial shade. Prefers evenly moist soil and blooms until frost arrives.

Cosmos (*Cosmos* spp., opposite, bottom row): A little happy pill of a flower. It's hard to be angry when you see something so pretty. I never get tired of this super easy and eager beauty that grows fast and produces many flowers. Cosmos do well in both pots and boxes a little larger than necessary, as they can get quite big. Feel free to trim it in midsummer if you want a stronger and denser flower bush. Loved by both insects and humans. Can be bought as a mature plant, but also sown from seed. I like to do both.

Marguerite daisy (*Argyranthemum* spp., above): Nothing compares. Hardy and faithful. I buy a couple every year and plant them together in a large plastic bucket. As long as you pluck off any wilted flower heads, this plant will bloom from early spring to late fall.

Geranium (*Pelargonium* spp., left). A classic that my grand-parents loved as much as I did. Easy to care for and can grow quite old if you make sure to take care of it, even just a little, every year. Available in countless varieties and color combinations. This one is my favorite with pink flowers and green leaves speckled with white. A flower you immediately notice in your outdoor space. I keep mine in the bedroom over the winter, where it's cool and frost-free.

Wandering purple heart (*Tradescantia pallida,* above): This one is for those of you looking for a bit of a different plant in your container garden. This is great as a houseplant all year round, but when it comes out in spring and summer, it turns dark purple and sprouts small pink flowers. This is super easy to grow cuttings from too. Cut off a couple of stems and plant them in wet potting soil in a sunny spot and you'll have a new dark-purple beauty among your pots. I bring mine indoors and keep it as a houseplant through the winter. This can also be propagated by putting the cuttings in water for a couple of weeks until it has developed roots, at which point it can be transplanted into moist soil after a month.

PROJECT 2: PERENNIALS AND EVERGREENS

Many cats can get a little drunk off sniffing catnip (left, center), hence the name. The most eager cats often roll over and into the catnip (unfortunately for you and your plant). The cats will then usually become either more relaxed or invigorated after their catnip-sniffing session. The degree of cat intoxication varies with the different varieties of catnip. Our cats Juni and Juli like having a sniff every now and then, but they don't have a catnip addiction just yet.

Perennials and evergreens will (hopefully) return year after year. They die back or go dormant in late fall, but come back to life when the spring sun peeks out. They thrive in the garden through summer and fall and then wither away again. And it's the same dance year on year. Think of it as a sleepy hibernation, and that they perk up when the sunlight and warmth return. They're like good friends who drop by during the summer break and bring you lots of joy. Parting is always a sad affair, but you know you'll see them again, and the joy of seeing each other may be even greater!

Summer flowers are an investment for the season, while perennials are an investment for life. That might sound like a bit of a stretch, but if you choose good perennials and look after them as you would good friends, they may well last for many years to come. A summer guest who drops by year after year. A wonderful reunion, pure and simple plant joy.

What You Will Need

Containers, soil, and a selection of your preferred perennials.

My Favorites for More Shaded Outdoor Spaces

- Hostas
- Cold-hardy ferns like male fern (*Dryopteris filix-mas*)
- Hydrangea

- Rodgers' bronze-leaf (*Rodgersia podophylla*)
- Maidenhair vine (*Muehlenbeckia complexa*)
- Elephant's ears (*Bergenia* spp.)
- Astilbe
- Bleeding heart (*Lamprocapnos spectabilis*, syn. *Dicentra spectabilis*)

My Favorites for More Sun-Exposed Outdoor Spaces

- Catnip (*Nepeta cataria*)
- Lavender (*Lavandula* spp.)
- Sage (*Salvia* spp.)
- Coral bells (*Heuchera sanguinea*)
- Small scabious (*Scabiosa columbaria*)

Care

Shade-Tolerant Perennials and Evergreens

Do you have an outdoor space with a lot or partial shade? I recommend hydrangea, hosta, ferns, and Rodgers' bronze-leaf (*Rodgersia podophylla*). These plants love moisture, so be generous with watering and choose plastic or glazed pots, as these retain moisture well. Their hardiness levels do vary but there are species that can tolerate temperatures as low as −30°F/−34.4°C, like *Hydrangea arborescens* and *H. paniculata*. They often like a bit of acidity in the soil, so consider using or mixing ericaceous compost into the pot or using a potting soil especially formulated for acid-loving plants.

Hosta and cold-hardy ferns are the safest choice and the most faithful perennials. Sometimes it can be nice to have friends who don't make too much of a fuss, but are always there for you, easy to be with, who pitch in but don't ask for much in return.

Hydrangea. Ooh-lala, is there a potted plant with a more impressive head of flowers? The hydrangea can grow over six feet/two meters tall if it is well cared for and kept in a large pot. It can withstand the winter outdoors if you live in milder areas, but if you live somewhere colder, I recommend that you keep the plant inside if you want it to flower again next year. Do you have those friends who take up quite a lot of space and are perhaps a bit much, but who at the same time spread a lot of life and joy around them? The hydrangea is bulky, so if you have a smaller outdoor space, you should bear in mind that it will take up a fair amount of room. A slightly more demanding and vain friend to hang out with, but who is also fascinating and who you just can't get enough of. These gorgeous flower globes will blossom throughout the summer as long as you prune away the dead flowers. This plant loves acidic soil, so feel free to use ericaceous compost. The hydrangea likes a lot of water, moisture, and nutrition, like most other large-flowering plants in the garden.

Rodgers' bronze-leaf is hardy in zones 5 to 7 and can thrive in larger planters or pots, preferably in partial or complete shade. It grows huge green leaves that have a bronze-like tinge. This plant is growing on me (and in my home) and has become one of the coolest plants in my potted plant gang.

Sun-loving perennials like well-drained soil. Feel free to mix sand, LECA, or gravel into the soil. I often use one-quarter drainage aids and three-quarters soil in the mix. Here, I've planted catnip in a steel planter.

Sun Lovers: Drought-Resistant Perennials and Evergreens

Is your outdoor space in a sunny location, or are you not too fond of spending all your time watering? My outdoor space gets a lot of sun, so I've opted for several sun-loving varieties that can withstand a period of dryness and hours of sunlight. My favorites are catnip (*Nepeta cataria*), lavender (*Lavandula* spp.), sage (*Salvia* spp.), small scabious (*Scabiosa columbaria*), and coral bells (*Heuchera sanguinea*). What these plants have in common is that they require little nutrition, can often withstand the winter outdoors, and like lots of sun and well-drained soil mixed evenly with plenty of drainage materials. They do not like too much shade or moist, heavy, and wet soil over time. If you live somewhere with a lot of rainfall, it's a good idea to make use of lots of drainage material, for example, LECA, to help get rid of excess water if it rains a lot. I personally tend to mix a lot of sand into my pots.

Small scabious is available in different varieties of pink or mauve. Its hardiness range is from zone 5a to 9b; it does well in my lovely container garden.

Lavender. Remember to water the soil around the plant, not over it, otherwise you risk the plant becoming too moist and moldy. If you live in a colder climate, choose English lavender (*Lavandula angustifolia*; I particularly like *L. angustifolia* 'Hidcote'), which can withstand extreme frost.

Coral bells. In my experience, this plant thrives best in a pot, rather than in a bed. It can thrive in hardiness zones 3 to 8 and is easy to care for. It is beautiful in late fall, especially placed by your front door or on the porch, and can tolerate some frost. With its various color combinations and different leaf sizes and shapes, coral bells are perfect for interplanting.

Good to Know

Hydrangeas can change color depending on the acidity of the soil. The blue hydrangea doesn't like lime, which is a challenge here in Hadeland, as our water is rich in lime. That means that our hydrangeas always turn pink, even if they start off blue. If you want blue hydrangeas more than anything, you can add aluminum sulfate. White hydrangeas, however, do not change color.

CONTAINER FACT

Good choices for perennial climbing plants include clematis, Boston ivy, Virginia creeper (*Parthenocissus* spp.), and common hops (*Humulus lupulus*). Choose large pots, planters, or boxes for these plants, as they can all get quite big, and some can be invasive (a little research can save you a lot of trouble!). These can be easily cut and pruned down if they get too large and long. Some climb by themselves, while others (like clematis) need a little help to latch onto something. I tend to place the pot against a trellis or wall and use steel wire to guide the plant. Secure the plant with steel wire, rope, or twine as it grows upwards.

PROJECT 3: ORNAMENTAL GRASS

There's almost nothing more beautiful than an elegant ornamental grass dancing in the wind; in fact, wind and grass are a great combination. I have a few large ornamental grass varieties that grow six feet/several meters high, and others that are smaller and a bit more modest.

What You Will Need

Your choice of ornamental grasses. I recommend selecting those that are hardy in your USDA zone. One or more pots or boxes. Soil and good drainage aids such as sand, gravel, or LECA.

Care

Most types of grass are hardy and require little care and supervision. They are often drought-resistant and require little nutrition. If necessary, consider providing them with some plant food in spring and midsummer.

How

Some grass types, such as pampas grass (*Cortaderia selloana*), have become particularly popular in recent years. In April, I bought pampas grass online, had three lots delivered, and planted them together in a large pot. They grew five times their size through the season, and I hope they'll thrive next year, and grow even bigger and more beautiful. They can survive outside in zones 8 to 10; I overwinter mine indoors. Pampas grass isn't

the easiest ornamental grass to succeed with, but I really want the pompous white pampas in my outdoor space. They thrive in a lot of sun and well-drained soil, so I've mixed some sand and gravel into the potting soil.

Good to Know

Ornamental grass is almost as beautiful in fall, and in winter as well. The effect is magical when the strands of grass and straw are covered with light snowflakes, and even better when they sparkle in the white frost, which we have a lot of here in Hadeland.

CONTAINER TIP

Do you live somewhere exposed to a lot of wind? If you answered yes, ornamental grasses can be a great choice for your container garden, as they won't break easily in the wind, but rather dance with it. I see more and more balconies, roof terraces, and green areas in cities with planters full of ornamental grasses. Beautiful, and easy to care for.

PROJECT 4: PAPYRUS

Plants go through trends, just like clothes and music. Now this guy here has been the plant of choice for a couple years now. Papyrus (*Cyperus papyrus*) originates from Egypt and the Arabian Peninsula. It's not a particularly beautiful plant, but it is interesting in its own way. It has a few characteristics that make it a fun potted plant to have in your outdoor space.

What You Will Need

Papyrus cuttings, a pot (preferably one without holes), and potting soil. It can also be sown from seed or bought mature.

Care

This plant loves water and cannot be overwatered (which is the most common cause of death for most other potted plants). So, in other words, go wild! Papyrus unashamedly laps it all up. That means you can use a pot with no drainage hole so the plant can bathe in water. If the pot has a hole in the bottom, you can place it in a pond or a larger container of water. Papyrus likes full sun to partial shade. Bring it in during the winter, and it'll make a brilliant houseplant. Papyrus can also spend the winter frost-free under grow lights.

How

Papyrus is easy to propagate; just stick the head of the plant in water or wet soil. Leave it there for a month, then roots will sprout from the head. If you propagate it by putting cuttings in water, plant it in soil when the shoots underwater have grown to

about 2 to 4 inches/5 to 10 cm long. I recommend doing this in spring or winter, as the sun and heat make the roots grow faster. This can be achieved by putting the cuttings on a windowsill inside if there is a risk of frost or outdoors in the summer.

Good to Know

Papyrus provides great cuttings as gifts for the plant lovers in your life. Gift as a cutting in a nice bottle or in a small pot with wet soil.

CONTAINER TIP

Two tips about papyrus: The first is that it's great to cut and add as a decoration to vases alongside your other cut flowers. The second is that papyrus loves to drink water. For that reason I recommend planting it in a pot with no hole at the bottom. Papyrus often grows on riverbanks, such as the Nile in Egypt. It is an ancient plant that was used to make paper. Papyrus grows fast, so within a year or two it may well be as tall as me—perfect if you like your plants on the taller side!

PROJECT 5: VERVAIN HEAVEN

Ever been to paradise? Unless you live in gorgeous countryside, few of us have seen those pearly gates. I would, however, still like to claim that I have a little patch of heaven in the middle of my container garden. Vervain is a giant of a flower that reaches a little closer to the sky than the other potted plants. Yes, I'm talking about the giant vervain, which has become extremely popular in recent years, for several reasons. There's something ballerina-like about it, with its tall, slender stems, graceful flowers, and the way it sways in the wind. This is a jaw-dropper of an outdoor plant and certainly steals the show—you're sure to notice it as it towers high above the other summer flowers, with its lovely mauve color, as it moves beautifully in the wind, like it's waving to you. Now, I might sound a bit crazy, but that's just how excited I am about it, and how much I've fallen in love with this stunning plant. You too can cultivate your own giant vervain, and here are my tips for doing so.

CONTAINER FACT

Trend Alert!

Vervain is a fantastic plant and giant vervain is currently its most popular variety. Here are three of my favorites from left: Giant vervain (*Verbena bonariensis*), common vervain (*V. officinalis*), and lemon verbena (*Aloysia citrodora*).

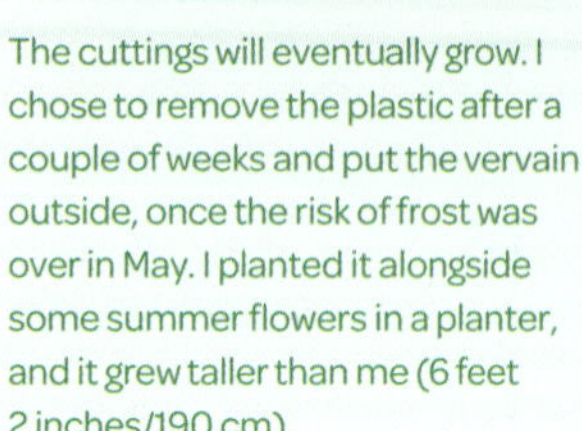

The cuttings will eventually grow. I chose to remove the plastic after a couple of weeks and put the vervain outside, once the risk of frost was over in May. I planted it alongside some summer flowers in a planter, and it grew taller than me (6 feet 2 inches/190 cm).

What You Will Need

A pot with soil, a saucer, cuttings, and a plastic bag.

How

- Plant five or six cuttings about 6 inches/15 cm apart in potting soil. Remove any leaves from the lower part of the cutting before sticking the cutting about 2 inches/5 cm deep in the soil.
- Some people like to cut an inch or so/a couple cm off of the top shoot, so that the cutting uses all its energy to take root. I always forget to cut the top, but it usually goes well.
- Pack the soil carefully around the cuttings so that they stand firmly, and then water the soil.
- Now put a transparent plastic bag over the pot. Make a small hole in the plastic, so that you don't end up with too much moisture inside the bag, otherwise there's a risk of the cuttings developing mold.

- Put the pot on a saucer and place it in a window that gets bright light.
- Check that it is moist every so often, but in my experience, minimal watering is needed. The minigreenhouse you have made usually retains enough moisture.

Care

Giant vervain prefers somewhere with full sun but can also thrive in partial shade. It will want consistent moisture, so the potting soil should be watered regularly. It likes well-drained soil, so feel free to mix LECA, sand, or pebbles into the pots. Giant vervain can grow 3 to 6 feet/1 to 2 meters high if you give it good, nutrient-rich soil and, ideally, extra plant food a couple of times throughout the spring and summer. This plant can also tolerate some frost and spend the winter indoors under grow lights.

I pruned this giant vervain in fall and overwintered it frost-free under grow lights in the basement. I then took lots of cuttings from it in spring. This plant became a father to five other giant vervains as a result. Next year, there will be at least ten new vervain babies. You can sow gaint vervain early in the spring (the seeds are a little difficult to germinate), and propagate it by cuttings, or buy a new one every year at your local nursery or garden center.

I also tried to propagate vervain with cuttings in water, but this didn't really work, and they just went a bit moldy. So if you do want to propagate vervain with cuttings in water, you should change the water weekly and leave the cuttings in a glass in a sunny window. My experience is that it is easier to succeed with cuttings in soil in the minigreenhouse than in water.

Good to Know

Giant vervain originally comes from South America, where it is a perennial plant, but since it cannot withstand Norway's cold freezes, it must be wintered indoors.

If you fancy growing other types of vervain, try common (*Verbena officinalis*) or lemon (*Aloysia citrodora*). Our common vervain was beautiful until our chickens found out they loved it and ate it all up while I slept in the hammock...

If giant vervain breaks a twig, don't despair. Clip the broken branch down to about 2 inches/5 cm above the base. New fresh shoots will often then sprout from the breakage. In addition, you can try using the broken branch as a cutting in wet soil or as a beautiful cut flower in a vase.

CONTAINER TIP

Vervain is beautiful as a cut flower in a vase, preferably together with other summer flowers from your container garden. I personally think it goes well with yellow flowers.

PROJECT 6: BLOOM BONANZA

From teeny tiny seeds to abundant blooms—sow the seeds directly into your pots and planters.

By *bloom bonanza* I mean a flower explosion in your container garden. It's hard to imagine how such small seeds can turn into such magnificent flowers that your neighbors are sure to notice. Sowing seeds in large pots and boxes is underrated and can give you a fireworks display of colorful blossoms in your outdoor space. It's also budget-friendly, giving you a lot of blooms for your buck.

What You Will Need

Seeds from your favorite plants (and if you don't have any yet, see my tips below), a pot or planter that already has soil in it, and new soil, to top up your chosen container.

How

It is generally best to sow the seeds directly into the pots in the spring, when the risk of frost has passed and the temperature rises. The timing depends somewhat on where you live, but for us May is a good month—we have however also sown in June and July. The warmer it is outside, the faster the soil in the pots heats up, and germination accelerates.

Care

The seeds generally require little care. Many of these flower seed varieties are robust and can survive for long periods without water and plant food. Remember that all plants like regular access to water and nutrients, but some do better than others with less care and supervision, a bit like us humans. Flower

seeds love the sun but can also do well in partial shade. Feel free to mix different seed varieties for more colorful visuals. You can also use a ready-made mixture, which you will often find sold as a wildflower meadow mix.

Good Seeds to Sow Directly in Pots

- Poppies (*Papaver rhoeas*, *Eschscholzia californica*)
- Pot marigold (*Calendula officinalis*)
- Fiddleneck (*Phacelia tanacetifolia*)
- Cornflower (*Centaurea cyanus*)
- Nasturtium (*Tropaeolum majus*)
- Meadow flower mix

Poppies. I love both red common poppies (*Papaver rhoeas*) and orange California poppies (*Eschscholzia californica,* top left).

Fiddleneck (*Phacelia tanacetifolia,* middle left) is often used as a field plant where I live to bind nutrients in the soil, otherwise known as green manure, which is great for ensuring healthy soil. It also works well in larger boxes and planters. This mauve flower germinates quickly, grows tall, and attracts an enormous number of beneficial organisms, including butterflies and bees. It does well when cut back if you think it is getting too high or starting to sag. The fiddleneck is drought-resistant and requires minimal food and care. In winter, it can be allowed to wither down and remain in the pots to nourish the soil for the next year.

Nasturtium (*Tropaeolum majus,* bottom left). Another splash of color for those who favor the vibrancy of yellow, orange, and red. Nasturtium grows quickly and spreads outwards. It is edible and perfect as a ground cover if you have trees in larger pots. You can let this flower grow and spread itself, or you can guide it upward along a fence, trellis, or wall. Cut it down if you think it's getting too bulky.

CONTAINER TIP

Did you think you have to throw away your old potting soil every year? No need! Especially in larger pots and boxes, you can certainly reuse the soil and sow the next season's flower seeds into it, which will explode into beautiful blooms throughout the summer. Many flower seeds do well in barren, used soil.

Clean away last year's plant remains from the pots and turn the soil over a little with a spade to loosen it up a bit. Push the seeds into the soil (about 1 to 1½ inches/3 to 4 cm deep) or spread the seeds out and cover with a thin ½- to ¾-inch/1- to 2-cm layer of soil. Check the seed pack for the recommended depth the seeds should be sown as well as how far apart they should be from one another.

Water thoroughly so that the seeds get enough moisture to germinate. Moisture also binds the seeds to the soil and keeps them from blowing away. Keep the soil evenly moist for the first few weeks for good germination.

Containers in the Spring

Good to Know

Get one or more varieties of seeds. I like having one type of variety in each pot, for instance, a pot of poppies and a box of fiddleneck (*Phacelia tanacetifolia*) every year. You can also try mixing different flower seeds in a larger box, or buy a meadow flower mix, but be aware that certain varieties can take over and become dominant, such as nasturtium and fiddleneck.

Pot marigold (*Calendula officinalis,* above left) is easy to grow and also happens to be edible. If you like to garnish your food with flowers, the pot marigold is tasty and decorative. It is also adaptable and does well in full sun to partial shade. This flower likes even moisture and good, nutrient-rich soil, so this can receive slightly more enriched soil or plant food than the other flowers.

PROJECT 7: SUNFLOWERS

I love sunflowers (*Helianthus annuus*), the garden's happiest flower. Try being mad while looking at a sunflower. Exactly, you can't—it brings out a wide smile and a feeling of warmth in most of us. In addition, sunflowers are easy to sow and grow, and they look just as good in pots as in beds or as part of a small meadow in your garden. Sunflowers are inexpensive, you get a LOT of flower for your money, and insects love them. Good for both the wallet and the environment. Dreaming of a small yellow oasis of sunflowers? You'll find my best tips below.

What You Will Need

Nutrient-rich soil, a pot, sunflower seeds, and some nutrient such as composted cow manure or liquid plant food.

How

- One seed in each container will do. Even if I plant two seeds, I know for sure that one of them will germinate. If you soak the sunflower seeds in water for a day before sowing, they'll be softer and germinate faster.
- Make a small depression in the soil with your finger, about 1 to 2 inches/3 to 5 cm deep, drop the seed in, and cover with soil. Some swear by potting soil, but I think it works best to sow them in soil formulated for flowers. The latter also has more nutrition for strong, early growth for the plant. I recommend ensuring there are holes in the bottom of the container to drain excess water.

CONTAINER FACT

Sunflowers are the national flower of Ukraine, and the country is known for its vast sunflower fields. Sunflowers have become a symbol and reminder of Ukraine's struggle for freedom. There is a high probability, in fact, that the seed you plant in your garden comes from Ukraine.

- To speed up germination, you can leave the container somewhere warm for a couple of days, for example, on a bathroom floor or in a sunny window. You can also cover the top of the pot with plastic wrap for a kind of greenhouse effect. When you see the sprouts coming out of the soil after one or two weeks, you can remove the plastic.

Sowing Directly into Pots

You can sow sunflower seeds directly into pots in May, when the danger of frost is over. They germinate faster if the pot is kept in a warm, bright place, for example, in a sunny corner of your outdoor space, as potting soil is heated faster by the spring sun than soil in the ground. The more the soil warms up in the spring, the faster the sunflower seeds will germinate, and you'll see earlier and better sunflower growth. Remember to maintain even moisture in the soil. Consider repotting the sunflower in a larger container if it gets particularly big. It also depends on how big you want your sunflowers to get!

How about wearing a flower in your shirt pocket from your own container garden? Natural and eye-catching—you're guaranteed to get noticed!

Our sunflower 'Teddy Bear' here was sown in April. It was then transplanted into a large pot filled with nutrient-rich potting soil in May. Watered well after planting, the pot was placed in a sunny, warm spot and periodically was given additional plant food to encourage good growth and large flowers. I mixed in some sand to make the pot a little heavier, making sure it stood steady as the sunflower grew taller and taller. Sunflowers come in many different colors and are loved by bees. Our neighbor produces honey, so our sunflowers are constantly visited by eager workers from the garden next door. And the honey tastes heavenly: sweet and delicious.

Indoor Cultivation

I sow sunflowers indoors in my sunny kitchen window about four to five weeks before planting in pots, typically in April. Then I plant my small sunflower plants into larger pots outdoors in mid-May, when the danger of frost is over. This timing, of course, depends on where you live. If you have a sunny corner in your outdoor space, this will be a perfect place for your newly planted sunflowers, but be aware that they can get sunstroke and sunburn. You should therefore acclimate them to the sun gradually during the first few weeks. The advantage of starting indoors with precultivation is that the sunflowers get a head start, so they bloom earlier, and you can enjoy these happy yellow flowers for longer. In other words, more flower joy and food for your container garden fever.

Care

Sunflowers love the sun! They should be planted in full sunlight but can tolerate partial shade. Give them plant food in the form of composted cow manure as a top layer over the existing soil or add liquid fertilizer mixed into water if you want large and glorious sunflowers that grow well throughout the summer months. I like to give my sunflowers extra plant food a couple of

CONTAINER TIP

How about trying a variety of sunflower other than the classic one we all know and love? Sunflowers come in a wide array of types, colors, and sizes. Some are gigantic and can grow to be many feet/meters high, while others stay on the smaller side.

times a month, especially in July and August. I use homemade liquid plant food made from nettles (nettle water) or fertilizer in the form of chicken pellets. Little growth and few flowers are the signs of a nutrient deficiency. Sunflowers can tolerate some drought, but if you want to remain on their good side, ensure the soil stays evenly moist with regular watering, unless you live somewhere with a lot of rainfall.

Good to Know

Sunflowers are native to North America but have become widespread and popular throughout Europe. Sunflowers did not get their name because of their sunny yellow color, but because the flowers face the sun. An eye-catching plant in the garden that you will certainly notice.

Invite the kids to help out with the sunflowers! They grow quickly, and it's a great source of fun for them to follow the growth of their own sunflower. In Norway some municipalities and schools have sunflower competitions to see, come fall, who ends up with the tallest sunflower. Or maybe you could challenge your neighbors to a sunflower competition?

PROJECT 8: POPCORN GRASS

Corn (*Zea mays*) is an annual cereal plant in the grass family (Poaceae) and is considered the world's most important grain. But did you know that unpopped popcorn can become an incredibly beautiful ornamental grass in your outdoor space? Popcorn grass has been megapopular on social media, and more and more people are jumping on the trend. It is especially beautiful as this large and voluminous grass transports you away to scenes of the countryside, with the tall corn grass swaying playfully in the wind. Popcorn grass is super easy, very decorative, cheap, and a fun project for both children and adults alike.

What You Will Need

Unpopped popcorn, potting soil, and a plant pot.

Care

Popcorn grass does well in regular potting soil. It likes regular watering and even moisture. If you want a big, beautiful stand of grass, add plant food (see pages 80–81) two to three times a month during the growing season, from June to September. It prefers a sunny spot but can also do well in partial shade.

How

I filled a container with potting soil in mid-June and sprinkled unpopped popcorn kernels on top. I used two handfuls of kernels and spread these out in a large pot. I sowed the kernels close together to achieve a thick, massive plant. I then covered the popcorn with a thin layer of soil (¾ to 1 inch/a couple of cm deep), watered the soil well, and put the pot outside in a warm, sunny spot. If you first soak the hard corn kernels in water for a day, they will become softer and germinate faster.

Corn kernels + soil + water + solar heat = popping in the pot after one to two weeks.

Day 10

Day 17

Day 30

Within a couple of weeks, germination was well underway. The popcorn grass grew well into the fall and only died when the frost came in October. I will definitely be doing this again next year!

Good to Know

The warmer it is, the faster germination starts. Make sure the soil doesn't dry out; keep it evenly moist.

PROJECT 9: TREES AND SHRUBS

I think trees in containers look elegant and impressive. They tower over the other potted plants and create a mini park or forest feeling in your own outdoor space, whether you live on the ground floor or high up in an apartment building. In addition, trees help to divide the outdoor space, provide a kind of privacy screen, and create a more sheltered zone for the other potted plants, as they provide added protection from the wind. Many trees grow well in pots and can thrive for years.

What You Will Need

A tree of your choice that you like and that suits your style and climate, and a larger pot with some weight, so it can keep the tree steady even if it's windy. Good nutrient-rich soil and plant food, when necessary. Drainage aids in the form of LECA or gravel. Plant stakes.

Care

Most trees like water and nutrients.

How

If you plant a newly acquired tree in a new pot, give it space by using a larger pot, as it will have more room for its growing roots. As the tree eats up the nutrients in the soil, add additional plant food. As it is rather cumbersome to repot larger trees, instead of changing the soil, you can make the soil airier by sticking a spike into the soil around the tree every spring, and adding a good layer of fresh nutrient-rich soil on top, for example, soil formulated for flowers, compost soil, or composted cow manure.

Good to Know

A tree that grows slowly rarely breaks at the root. It is a good idea to choose slow-growing trees—so-called dwarf or mini varieties—for pots. A huge fir tree that grows 50 feet/15 meters high, for example, won't be suitable for your container garden. Smaller varieties of trees and ornamental shrubs thrive in large pots, such as white spruce (*Picea glauca*), dwarf mountain pine (*Pinus mugo*), Young's weeping birch (*Betula pendula* subsp. *pendula* 'Youngii'), and my favorite, weeping Japanese larch (*Larix kaempferi* 'Pendula'), are more suitable.

There are a number of apple trees that grow well in pots, such as columnar apples, which are more slow-growing. Ask your local garden center for tips.

Because they're taller, trees are more exposed to wind. You should therefore choose a heavier pot made of clay, concrete, or cast iron, or fill the bottom of the pot with gravel or pebbles before repotting. That way, the tree will keep its balance. You can tie your tree to a support stake in the first year to help it establish itself, get a good root system going, and better withstand the wind.

CONTAINER TIPS

Do you get a lot of wind in your outdoor space? Choose trees with less and finer foliage. That way, if the wind picks up, you'll avoid the leaves being blown to pieces.

Some trees can withstand the winter outside in pots, such as pines. Others you will need to check the hardiness level of, such as this willow-leaved pear (*Pyrus salicifolia,* opposite), which also goes by the name of the Nordic olive tree. It's cold-hardy in zones 4 to 7. I overwinter mine indoors or put it somewhere sheltered and keep my fingers crossed.

A tree that grows upside down. I myself love hanging trees and by that I mean trees where the crown hangs down, such as a dwarf weeping willow (*Salix,* top), shown here, with wild pansies as ground cover. It's a good idea to plant some small summer flowers under larger trees and shrubs in your containers—this means that the soil will not be as exposed to the sun and retains moisture better.

Japanese maple (*Acer palmatum,* bottom) has become a classic potted plant, thanks to its unusual colors, beautiful appearance, and the fact that it is easy to care for. If it is placed somewhere sheltered, it will have great foliage. If it is exposed to a lot of strong winds, the foliage can suffer quite a bit of damage and end up looking a little mottled.

Continued

Continued from previous page

Dwarf mountain pine (*Pinus mugo,* opposite, top left) does well in pots. It is hardy, evergreen, and can manage outdoors in many climates. I also like the magical bonsai feeling it evokes.

Trees in containers are really beautiful in an urban environment characterized by concrete (opposite, top right). The contrast is great, and you get a reminder of how important trees and nature are to us humans. Yes to greener urban spaces with more trees!

Rhododendrons (opposite, bottom left) are evergreen and bloom in early spring. They thrive in pots. Rhododendrons like even moisture and acidic soil, so feel free to use ericaceous compost. You can also use regular potting soil and make the soil more acidic by adding coffee as plant food or adding a layer of pine needles to the soil.

"Evergreen trees are beautiful all year round and risk turning your neighbors green with envy."

Lilacs (*Syringa* spp., opposite, bottom right) come in many varieties and are well suited to containers. Or how about a red currant bush (*Ribes rubrum*)? Many of the shrubs we think of as traditional garden shrubs can also be decorative and thrive in pots.

Boxwood (*Buxus sempervirens,* left) is a hardy evergreen. It looks great at entrances to houses and other buildings. You can see it here in a pot sprayed with gold Bengalack lacquer. Perhaps not for everyone, but certainly for those of us who enjoy a bit of bling in our outdoor space.

CONTAINER TIP

Are you sick of the same old look of your containers? I love my terra-cotta pots for how they allow the colors to pop, but sometimes, after washing my pots, I like to spray them with Bengalack lacquer in one of my favorite colors: gold, bronze, or navy blue.

Many trees, such as ginkgo (*Ginkgo biloba*), are deciduous, which means they shed their leaves in the fall. The ginkgo is one of the oldest tree species in the world, its lineage going back 200 million years. The leaves return in the spring when the tree comes to life again for a new season.

Pruning Trees and Shrubs

How much you will need to trim and prune your trees and shrubs varies between different types. Some grow back quickly, others more slowly. Some are easy to cut to shape, others more complicated. A general trim can be carried out as follows:

- It is best to prune in early spring before the leafing process begins or in the fall after the leaves have shed, but before the frost arrives. It is generally fine to trim trees and shrubs in the summer too but spring and fall are recommended.
- Cut off any dead or damaged branches. Mostly healthy branches can be left as they are.
- Cut away crossing branches or branches that are too long and overgrown compared to the rest of the tree or shrub.
- Prune up to 25 percent of the plant; cutting more than that could damage it.
- Make sure to prune the plant with clean equipment. Blunt or dirty pruning tools can lead to wounds and damage that can be attacked by bacteria and fungi, which can further harm the tree.

If you want to prune the tree or shrub into a certain shape, you can cut into the middle of a branch if, for example, you want to make a round crown. However, the healthiest thing for the tree is to cut a couple of inches/cm away from what is called the branch collar, so that you don't damage the trunk.

PROJECT 10: BULBS AND TUBERS

Both bulbous and tuberous plants can offer a lovely display in your garden. The bulb-based tulip plant is spring's most beautiful sensation, and the tuberous dahlia is the flamboyant highlight of summer and fall!

What You Will Need

A selection of bulbs and/or tubers, a pot with a hole in the base, and soil.

My Favorite Bulbs and Tubers

- Tulip (*Tulipa* spp.)
- Daffodil (*Narcissus* spp.)
- Grape hyacinth (*Muscari* spp.)
- Dahlia (*Dahlia* spp.)
- Begonia (*Begonia* spp.)
- Gladiola (*Gladiolus* spp.) (strictly speaking, it grows from a corm)
- False shamrock (*Oxalis triangularis*) (propagated from a rhizome, an underground stem that grows horizontally, sending out shoots)

Care

Bulbs basically have all the nutrition they need contained within the bulb, so they don't need much in the way of nutritional amendments to the soil or additional feed. They do, however, require well-drained soil, so feel free to mix in a lot of drainage aids such as sand or LECA. Bulbs like full sun to partial shade.

Tuberous plants do initially have all the nutrition they need to germinate and grow, but as they sprout and develop, those that flower abundantly, like dahlias and begonias, will need a lot of water and nutrition. If you see their leaves turn pale and if they have few flowers, these are signs of a nutrient deficiency and you should give them plant food (see chapter 3). Tubers prefer to be in warm soil and full sun. They can cope with partial shade, but they will bloom a little later in the season and a little less.

How

Cold-hardy bulbs are planted at the end of the growing season—from the beginning of September to the beginning of November, depending on the hardiness zone. Bulbs can withstand some frost, but must have time to take root before the winter cold sets in. They should be planted close together with the tip pointing up and placed quite deep in the pot. Cover with about 4 inches/10 cm of soil. Water them a little so that the soil becomes moist and the bulbs will sprout roots. Cover the newly planted pot with leaves and place it snug against the wall of the house or in a nook. It's also a good idea to water them a little in the spring if the soil is dry, so that the plant remains slightly moist for growth and germination.

Tubers: I plant different tubers in containers every year. I either do this indoors in March, so-called precultivation, and then repot them outside when the danger of frost is over at the end of May, or I plant them directly into pots when the danger of frost has passed. The advantage of precultivating tuberous plants indoors is that you give the tuber a head start. Its flowers then bloom earlier and you can enjoy these floral sensations throughout the summer and fall.

Place the tubers in a water bath for a couple of hours and up to a day before planting them. The tuber will absorb water and sprout faster. I use ordinary potting soil and put the newly planted tuber somewhere warm and cozy, like a sunny nook. The soil then heats up, and the tuber sprouts faster. Remember to keep the soil evenly moist, but not soaking wet, as this can cause the tuber to rot.

Dahlias remain in bloom right up to when the frost sets in. In our garden, they often hang around well into the fall, until the October cold takes them. When frost is forecasted, you can dig up the tuber, brush or rinse it off so it's free of soil, and let it dry for a couple of days. Once dry, put it in a box or paper bag in a dark and preferably cool but frost-free place through the winter. Mine are kept frost-free in a cupboard in the basement.

Good to Know

Tulips often bloom in April/May, with the flowers lasting five to six weeks. While technically perennial, most modern hybrid tulips don't always come back on their own year after year. For that reason, many people plant new tulip bulbs every year as an annual project. However, you can try encouraging the tulip to bloom again the next year by cutting off the seed capsule and flower after it has finished flowering and giving it some plant food. Otherwise, you can do as I do and plant species tulips (also called botanical tulips); though slightly smaller, they are considered true perennials and sprout much more reliably year after year.

Dahlia tubers can last for many years if you overwinter them indoors. If you're feeling brave, you can leave the dahlias in the frost for a couple of days. This is beneficial as the nutrients from the plant find their way down into the tuber. I have done this several times. After a couple of days out in the cold, I dig them up, rinse them of soil, dry them indoors for a couple of days, and store them in a dark, frost-free spot in a basement or garage.

If you have the time and opportunity, you can curate large pots filled with tulips in your favorite colors. A project for next spring, perhaps?

Find inspiration in other people's gardens and from your travels! We are lucky enough to have friends with houses in Tuscany who plant tulip bulbs every year. I love how the tulips and other spring flowers start in February. By the time we get home, it's our turn here in Norway, as the spring sun warms up the tulip bulbs in April and May!

A lot of fun in a diminutive package. From a small tuber to 5-foot-/ 1.5-meter-high dinner-plate dahlias!

CONTAINER TIP

The more warmth and sun bulbs and tubers receive in the spring, the earlier they will sprout and bloom. Setting them in a sunny corner is therefore the ideal placement. And don't forget that tuberous flowers like being cut for use in bouquets or decorations. Just cut the flower stems, place them in vases, and carefully pluck/cut off any dead flower buds. If you cut and prune the dahlia plants regularly, they will quickly grow new shoots and rejuvenate themselves. You will be rewarded with fresh new flowers throughout the summer and fall.

Tuberous begonias are underrated, in my opinion. These days, they are available in many different types, and I particularly like the pink and yellow varieties. Begonias like consistent moisture and good nutrition throughout the summer for maximum flower splendor. The tubers can live for many years if you dig them up and protect them over the winter, somewhere frost-free and dark.

The **gladiola** (right) is particularly befitting of cut flowers in a tall vase and, in my experience, is one of the easiest plants to succeed with. Gladioli grow from small corms that are easy to plant, dig up, and store through the winter. Gladioli grown in containers often need some support to keep from toppling forward, so feel free to stake them as they grow.

Spring is on its way. The **false shamrock** (*Oxalis triangularis,* left) looks up expectantly and reaches for the spring light after a long winter's sleep. I don't dig up its rhizomes, but when the plant dies back in the fall, I take the whole container and put it in a cool, frost-free spot indoors through the winter. In the spring, I take the pot out again and put it somewhere bright and warm, either indoors for a period or directly out into the sunlight, depending on the weather. Its rhizomes then come to life and shoot upward in the spring.

PROJECT 11: CACTI AND SUCCULENTS

I love houseplants. That's why I take a selection of my green indoor friends, such as my cacti and succulents, on a loooong sunny vacation every summer—all the way into my garden. You can have a mini cactus and succulent garden in your outdoor space from May to October or even longer, depending on the weather forecast and where exactly you live. As long as your outdoor space remains frost-free, these plants can have a swell time outdoors.

What You Will Need

A selection of cacti or succulents, clay pots (such as terra-cotta), and potting/cactus soil (or make your own soil mix of one part potting soil and four parts sand and/or LECA).

Care

Light: Native to deserts with scorching sun, cacti and succulents naturally love the sun but can also do well in partial shade.

Location: A warm, sunny spot, but the most important thing is to ensure some protection from rain and moisture. I have mine on a concrete terrace next to the south-facing wall of the house, the sunniest side, where they are also protected from most of the rain.

Temperature: They love hot sun and heat during the day, but they also like cooler nights. Now, we don't exactly get desert heat here in the countryside, but if you've been in the desert, you'll know that it also gets very cool at night, which is lucky, given the fluctuating summer temperatures where I live.

Moving your succulents outside for the summer? Remember to make it a gradual transition, as is being done in the photo, so that the plants don't get sunburned or suffer frost damage. I use fiber cloth for two or three weeks as a protection against strong sun and frost, before they can withstand full sun exposure. If necessary, they can be placed in partial shade for the first few weeks.

Water and moisture: Water sparingly, meaning, a couple of times a month during the hottest part of the summer. If it is a wet season and they are exposed to the summer rain, they do tend to withstand rainwater. If they are under a roof, they will need a little water. These plants are more likely to thrive in pots made of breathable clay, like terra-cotta pots, as plastic pots hold too much moisture in the soil, which they don't like.

Soil: Use soil with plenty of drainage, like one specially formulated for cactus. Ordinary soil isn't suitable for these plants, as it retains too much moisture. Cacti and succulents like sandy, nutrient-poor soil, just like that found in the deserts of the Southwest, so that when it rains, the water drains away quickly and the soil dries up faster.

Nutrition: Cacti and succulents need little plant food, as their native habitat is nutrient-poor soil consisting of a lot of sand. Consider giving them a small diluted dose of plant food one or two times during the summer months, for example, once at the turn of May/June when you put them out, and again at the beginning of August.

How

Propagating succulents is exceptionally easy.

- Fill a pot with a mixture of sand and potting soil or use potting soil especially formated for cactus.
- Cut a couple of branches off a succulent, such as a jade plant, 2 to 4 inches/5 to 10 cm long.
- Pluck off the bottom leaves, and stick the stem about 2 inches/5 cm deep in the soil mix.
- Water thoroughly and keep the soil consistently moist for the first few weeks, so that the roots grow. Feel free to use a spray bottle.

I propagate cuttings outdoors every spring and summer, but this can also be done indoors in early spring, for example, from March to May before you put them out. The succulent can remain for years in the same pot and soil. Plain and simple.

My Favorite Succulents

- Agave (*Agave* spp.)
- *Aloe vera*
- Jade plant (*Crassula ovata*)
- Senecio (*Senecio* spp.)
- Kalanchoe (*Kalanchoe* spp.)
- Tree aeonium (*Aeonium arboreum*)

This agave (previous page, bottom right) stands in its own rather pompous and aristocratic pot, a flea market find from beautiful Bornholm in Denmark for the equivalent of $28. By the way, did you know that tequila is made from agave?

Opposite: On holiday in Marrakech, Morocco, where I found inspiration from the cacti and succulent gardens on the city's many roof terraces.

CONTAINER TIP

Make your own soil mix for desert and succulent plants with a mixing ratio of four to one—I like to mix about four parts drainage material, for example, LECA or sand, to one part soil. The soil contains the nutrients the plants need.

Wondering if the succulents need water? Often the skin, i.e., the surface of the foliage, will shrink if there is too little water inside the plant itself, a bit like dehydrated human skin that becomes more wrinkled. Shrunken leaf surfaces are signs that you need to water the plant in order to increase the water pressure inside the stem and leaves. A tense and shiny leaf surface is a sign that the plant is getting enough water.

Buy a selection of small cacti and plant them together in a larger pot. This way, you can create a small desert landscape—in miniature! I'm a big fan of cowboy culture and old westerns. I have a cowboy hat and cacti, so now all I need is a horse, a leather vest, and an old Colt.

PROJECT 12: TOMATO JOY

Nothing is better than fresh tomatoes picked from plants grown in our own container garden—in a sun-heated pot, planted in potting soil, and topped with eggshells over a bed of composted cow manure. From plant to plate!

Is there anything more delicious than homegrown sun-ripened tomatoes? Please. Of course not. There really is something about the joy of food you grow yourself—extra satisfying and so healthy.

Why not try your hand at this tomato joy project? Tomatoes require some effort in terms of water and nutrition, but you can often harvest lots of tomatoes well into the fall.

What You Will Need

Tomato seeds if you're looking to grow your tomatoes from scratch (see Seed Propagation, page 92), or you can buy a mature tomato plant at a garden center or nursery. You will also need potting soil, a large pot, and plant food.

Care

The tomato is a greedy plant that requires lots of nutrition. If it is placed somewhere where it gets a lot of sun and heat, for example, in a sunny corner or in a greenhouse, you should add plant food one or two times a week. If the foliage looks pale and transparent, this is a sign of nutrient deficiency, and the plant will produce smaller and fewer tomatoes, in addition to generally growing more slowly. The tomato plant does not like to dry out, so you should ensure good watering that keeps the soil evenly moist. In the hottest and sunniest months that means

CONTAINER FACT

Research shows that we find greater pleasure from eating food that's homegrown.

watering several times a week, unless you have very large pots or an automatic watering system for your container garden (check out the new self-watering microdrip systems now available online).

How

Tomatoes can be grown both outdoors and in greenhouses. It is easier to succeed outdoors if you have a warm and sunny nook in your outdoor space, so that the tomatoes have enough sun and heat to ripen and become ready to eat. If you are lucky and have a greenhouse, this process will go even faster.

> "Growing tomatoes will drink and drink, so water them a lot!"

You should eventually repot the tomato plant in a larger pot, or add plenty of extra soil and plant food. We didn't use particularly large pots (around 1½ gallons/5.5 liters) and instead chose to add some plant food and water. A simple self-watering solution ensured enough water. The plastic pot we used for the tomatoes had a hole in the bottom and was placed in a larger bucket with no hole. This way, we watered the bucket, and then, through the pot's drainage hole, the tomato plant was able to absorb the desired amount of water. We made sure that there

CONTAINER TIP

Support the tomato plant as it grows so that it doesn't snap. We used sticks and tubes for the first few weeks, then moved on to attaching the tomato stem to the twine on the ceiling of our greenhouse. We used cable ties to attach its branches to the twine and support stakes, so that it didn't break during the process.

Solanum lycopersicum, syn. *Lycopersicon esculentum*. Tomatoes come in many sizes, from small cherry tomatoes to large beefsteak tomatoes. They vary in color from red and yellow to brown and green. My favorites are the smaller cherry tomatoes, as these are extra sweet and ripen faster.

was always a couple of inches/cm of water at the bottom of the bucket. This meant that the tomato plant never dried out and always had regular access to water.

Remember to remove any *thieves* as the tomato grows. Thieves—or offshoots—must be removed as they steal nutrients from the plant, leading to lots of foliage and fewer tomatoes. Offshoots tend to be found in between the branch and the trunk (opposite, top left). You should be able to pinch these off easily with your fingers or, if necessary, they can be cut off too.

Tomatoes can be difficult to succeed with if they lack calcium. Eggshells contain a lot of calcium, so if you want to give your tomato plants a boost, crush eggshells and sprinkle a handful on top of the soil or, even better, mix them into the soil. Feel free to add eggshells three or four times during the growing season. The plants will gradually absorb the calcium from the shells. The eggshells also make the soil airier, which provides better drainage and encourages better root development. Another advantage is that snails and slugs apparently don't like their sharp edges, nor the smell. Just remember to rinse any leftover egg off the shell, so you don't get unwanted rodent visitors.

Nitrogen-rich plant nutrition leads to good growth. I used calcium nitrate mixed into water throughout the season (a small handful in a jug of 2½ gallons/9.5 liters of water, which should

CONTAINER TIP

If you prefer organic tomatoes, you have your pick of options for nutrition, from liquid gold and nettle water to composted livestock manure products. If you are wary about mixing livestock manure products into your edible plants, check out your local extension agency for more information.

be left to dissolve in the water for an hour before watering), so that the plant receives maximum nutrition and, thus, maximum tomato yield.

Gently shake the tomato plants (see photo, left) when the flowers appear. By doing this, you're helping them self-pollinate.

Good to Know

What if your tomatoes haven't ripened before the frost comes? Bring them inside and place them on a bright, sunny windowsill with the stem pointing up and they will usually ripen within a week or two.

CONTAINER FACT

Tomatoes are native to South America and were brought to Europe by Christopher Columbus. It wasn't until the nineteenth century that tomatoes became popular in Italy and a common food around the Mediterranean. In Northern Europe, tomatoes only became common after World War I.

PROJECT 13: POTATOES IN BUCKETS

CONTAINER TIP

Do not use ordinary potatoes from the grocery store for cultivation, as they can spread infection in the soil. Buy certified seed potatoes, either online or at a garden center.

The potato is as fresh and healthy as anything. This plant is easy to succeed with and, best of all, you'll get a lot in return for little effort. I think it's a particularly fun plant to harvest, and even more so with children—these pleasing tubers can be magically pulled up from the ground in large numbers. Hadeland, where I live, is known as the Potato County in Norway. We have rich soil over Cambro-Silurian deposits, which makes the land well suited for root vegetables. When Erik was at school here, they didn't call it the "fall break," but rather the "potato holiday," as the children of Hadeland would harvest hundreds of thousands of potatoes to the delight of dinner tables across Norway throughout the fall and winter.

What You Need

Seed potatoes, soil, and a planter or large pot with a hole in the bottom. We used two large food-scale plastic buckets into which we drilled drainage holes.

The seed potato is available as an *early season seed potato*, which is fresher, ripens earlier, and is harvested and eaten in the summer, preferably at a barbecue, while *late season seed potatoes* are harvested and eaten throughout fall and winter. So when you buy seed potatoes, check whether they are early or late season sets, depending on what you want. We went for the 'Kerrs Pink' variety, a late season potato. I would like to have potatoes for the summer, though, so next year I'll be doing early season potatoes instead. We're always trying something new here!

Care

The potato plant likes the sun—something the potato and I have in common. The bucket or planter should ideally be placed somewhere sunny after planting. Potatoes benefit from nutrient-rich soil, with two parts potting soil and one part compost or other plant food, so that they have some nutrition throughout the season (see pages 80–81). We just used soil from our own garden, which also worked well. (As I mentioned, our garden soil is ideal for growing potatoes.)

The potato plant likes even moisture. If the soil looks dry, stick your finger in and check if it feels wet. If it feels dry, you should water it. We watered our plant once or twice a week, but then we had a particularly rainy summer this year. If it is hot and dry, you may need to water more frequently. The advantage of plastic buckets is that plastic as a material retains moisture well, so you don't have to water as regularly.

CONTAINER TIP

Do you have lawn and grass clippings? Grass clippings work great as a top layer, as they provide nourishment for better potato growth and they help the soil retain more moisture, meaning you don't have to water them as often. Add about 4 inches/10 cm of grass clippings on top of the soil a couple of times during the season.

How

Check that the seed potatoes have visible sprouts, which means they have germinated, before you plant them. If they haven't germinated, leave them in the sunlight for a couple of weeks on a windowsill, for example, in an open egg carton. Spray them regularly with water, and the shoots will definitely sprout. Ours took a bit of time before we could plant them but it all turned out well in the end.

Seed potatoes should be planted outside when the danger of frost has passed, which, here in our part of Norway, means mid-May.

You can get up to fifteen potatoes from one seed potato, so if you choose to plant yours in smaller pots, for example in 2½- to 5-gallon/9.5- to 19-liter pots, make sure to just plant one seed potato in each pot. We used 16-gallon/60.5-liter buckets and put four seed potatoes in each.

Jerusalem artichokes (*Helianthus tuberosus*) are a great alternative to potatoes. They have edible tubers, thrive in pots and planters, and have exceptionally beautiful flowers!

Plant the potatoes about 8 inches/20 cm apart. If you plant them in a raised bed, you can place them in a row. Make a depression about 4 inches/10 cm deep, set the seed potato in the hole with the green sprout facing upwards, and cover with about 2 to 4 inches/5 to 10 cm of soil. Water thoroughly and place the pot in a sunny position for good growth.

After a couple of weeks, you will see the potato vines growing. When the vine is about 4 inches/10 cm high, *hilling* is recommended, which means piling about 2 inches/5 cm of soil up to and above the bottom half of the stem of the potato vine.

You can easily hill the soil in a planter or bucket by filling the container with an extra layer of about 2 to 4 inches/5 to 10 cm of soil on top. Then push the excess soil up around the stems.

Good to Know

When should you harvest potatoes? The potatoes will flower beautifully, and as the flowers die away, the vine will eventually begin to turn yellow. At this point they are ready for harvesting. Our neighbor, who is a potato farmer, harvests his late season potatoes at the end of September/beginning of October. We were early harvesting ours in August, so next time we'll wait until September. The advantage of planting potatoes in containers is that the soil warms up earlier than the ground, which helps them grow and ripen earlier.

CONTAINER FACT

The advantage of hilling is that it stimulates more growth, and the extra topsoil gives you more tubers and a bigger crop! You'll also keep the potato tubers from being exposed to the sun, which can turn them green, toxic, and inedible. On top of this, hilling also protects against pests. I forgot to hill the potatoes this year, but luckily they had enough soil, so it wasn't an issue.

PROJECT 14: ONIONS IN PLANTERS

Red and Yellow Onions

Yes, you may get a touch of onion breath, and, yes, you may shed a tear or ten when cutting into them, but both are outweighed by the versatility of the onion. Onions are a wonderful flavor enhancer in many different dishes and absolutely necessary in all sorts of sauces. And on top of all that, they are great for your health and packed with nutrients.

What You Will Need

Small onion sets (immature bulbs)—we planted red and yellow onion bulbs. A box or large pot/bucket and nutrient-rich soil. We used a simple planter that we placed directly on the ground. It is also a good idea to provide some extra nutrition/fertilizer throughout the growing season (see pages 80–81).

Care

Onions love the sun, so the planter should be put somewhere sunny. It likes and needs nutrition-rich soil. Mix in a bag of composted cow manure or other plant food when planting, and fertilize the soil a couple of times a month until it's time to harvest.

How

We used small yellow and red sets that we bought online. Sets are the easiest way to grow onions, but onions can also be sown from seed, it just takes longer.

We placed the planters in a sunny spot outside. A simple pallet frame for onions is often sufficient, as the roots don't dig down particularly deep. You could even place two pallet frames on top of each other.

The frame or planter can be placed directly on the ground, but in this instance, I would recommend a ground cover for the base. Otherwise, you will find that the bed may become quickly overgrown with weeds—something we experienced ourselves. This will mean a lot of weeding, which I'm not particularly fond of. The planter can also be placed on gravel, cement, or other material, but with a ground cover cloth underneath to help retain moisture and hold the soil in place, so that it doesn't spill out. We filled about one-third of each box with organic material at the bottom such as leaves, grass clippings, and small twigs.

It feels good reusing materials from the garden. Sustainable and economical—soil can be expensive. We then filled the planter with potting soil and mixed in a bag of composted cow manure to make the soil extra nutrient-rich. This ensures the onions get off to a good start. Bear in mind that the set doesn't like being in overly wet soil, so mix in some sand, gravel, or pebbles if you have any available. We used gravel from the driveway.

We waited until the danger of frost was over before putting them out, which is usually mid-May here, but it depends on where you live.

We planted the onion bulbs by sticking a finger into the soil. We made a row of holes down the length of the planter. The distance should be around 2 to 4 inches/5 to 10 cm between the onions or, if you have several rows, there should be around 8 to 12 inches/20 to 30 cm between each row, depending on the size of the onion. Shallots are somewhat larger. I mostly measure this by sight, and am not particularly precious about it, but it tends to go well! I put the onion bulbs in the holes at a depth of around 2 inches/5 cm, with the tips facing upwards. I then cover them with a thin layer of soil and water them thoroughly.

Good to Know

The onion is ready to harvest when the stem bends, withers, and becomes more yellow in color. Our onions tasted wonderful, but next time we plan on giving them more nutrition throughout the growing season, as they would probably have grown a little bigger.

Chives

If you don't have a particularly green thumb, go for chives (*Allium schoenoprasum*). I would argue that it is the easiest of the outdoor edible plants to succeed with. Once you've planted your chives, you'll have chives for life—regardless of whether they're in a pot or planter. We have chives in our beds. They are the first edibles to sprout in the garden and can be enjoyed as early as April. Chives thrive in smaller pots too. It's a super hardy plant and can generally spend the winter outdoors in more temperate regions, in all sorts of containers. Chives can be harvested and cut down several times during the season and used as a garnish for eggs, pasta, potatoes, and more. In contrast to onions, it is the upper part—the stem itself—that we eat on the chives. Buy a chive plant at your local nursery and plant it in your pot or planter in the spring. Otherwise, chives can be found in many gardens, and you can easily dig up a small plant and move it into your pots or boxes.

PROJECT 15: HERB GARDEN

EDIBLE PLANTS

Herbs have grown on me tremendously in recent years. They're easy to grow, are lovely to look at, smell great, and taste amazing! You can create your own herb garden with a selection of your favorite herbs in pots or beds. Plus, they're super healthy, and the knowledge of herbs and their healing medicinal properties goes back in human history for hundreds, if not thousands, of years. More and more people are opening their eyes to the magical properties of herbs. Herbs are great for cooking, in medicine, and as a drink.

What You Will Need

Potting soil formulated for flowers or Mediterranean or citrus plants, a selection of your favorite herbs, and pots or planters.

Care

Many herbs like a typically Mediterranean climate and prefer well-drained soil. I therefore mix a lot of sand (about one-quarter of the pot) into the soil. If you get a lot of rain where you live, the soil can be mixed with LECA, sand, or gravel for a more aerated and well-drained soil. Herbs love the sun, so they should be placed in a sunny spot. This means that they can manage in fairly barren soil and tolerate drought between waterings. You generally do not need to add that much plant food throughout the season, but if the foliage looks pale and loses its green color, you can top it up with new soil or add plant food (see chapter 3).

How

Herbs do well when planted together in larger pots or planters, ideally spaced at a distance of 6 to 16 inches/15 to 40 cm, depending on how large the herbs grow and whether they tend to spread out.

Water thoroughly when potting the plant for the first time. You can harvest the top shoots early, as this will lead to both more and faster growth. Harvest the top shoots regularly, a couple of times a month. The herbs will then grow steadily throughout the summer and into the fall—we enjoy homegrown herbs until the frost comes in October.

Good to Know

Some herbs can survive outdoors through the winter in milder climate zones. Some are cold-hardy; in my experience, oregano, thyme, and mint withstand the winter outdoors, but be aware that there are some herbs that do better than others. I have to plant new Greek oregano every year and am just as happy every time when I see it start to pop up in my herb box.

A SELECTION OF MY FAVORITE HERBS

Oregano (*Origanum* spp.) is definitely the herb we have the most of in our garden. It is suitable for many different types of cooking. If you can, I would recommend getting two or three oregano plants, or at least that is my experience from growing

---

CONTAINER TIP

Buy herbs from a proper nursery or good garden center. The herbs you buy in the grocery store are consumables, less hardy, and won't grow as well. They are therefore not suitable for your herb garden. There are many different varieties within just one type of herb, and the hardiness can vary, so check the variety name and google its hardiness level if you want varieties that can endure the winter where you live. You can also sow herb seeds indoors February through April and plant them out when the danger of frost is over. For this, you should use either grow lights or a sunny window.

Before and after. If I'm lucky, I can get started on planting the herb garden in early May when the frost is over. At that point, some of the survivors from the winter hibernation appear, and I plant out the rest of the herbs for the season. If you would like some flowers to accompany your herb garden, it can be nice to plant a few in between the herbs, such as carnations, small scabious, or dahlias.

Oregano, rosemary, and thyme

herbs over the years. Oregano goes well with pasta, halloumi, pizza, and all tomato-based dishes.

Thyme (*Thymus* spp.) is a delightful hardy plant that only just withstands the winter here in Hadeland. If you live in zone 4 or higher, it can stay outdoors in winter. Thyme is drought-
resistant, loves the sun, and tastes great in Italian food. It's available in many different varieties; my favorite is lemon thyme (*T. citriodorus*), which has a wonderful smell and tastes heavenly on pizza.

Sage (*Salvia officinalis*) is an exceptionally beautiful herb with its large, silvery gray foliage. I would vote for it as the prettiest herb, in addition to the fact that sage tastes fantastic with ravioli, butter, and parmesan. Sage can manage outside in milder climate zones in Norway, but it gets too cold for it here in Innlandet, and it dies if I don't move it inside for the winter.

Mint (*Mentha* spp.) comes in many types and varieties. If you have mint in your outdoor space, you will be sure to smell its characteristically sweet scent. I use mint to make tea. It also tastes great with food from the Middle East, for example, in a bulgur salad. It is generally recommended to plant mint by itself in a container, as it spreads quickly outward if planted directly in a bed or alongside other plants. Many types of mint can withstand the winter in Norway, so it will depend on which type you acquire. It is often enough to buy a single mint plant, as it grows and spreads quickly.

Rosemary (*Salvia rosmarinus*, syn. *Rosmarinus officinalis*) is excellent for those who love root vegetables, and I reguarly sprinkle it over baked potatoes and other vegetables. It also tastes incredible with lamb. Rosemary can grow into large

Mint is a wonderful herb for tea. Place a couple of mint leaves in hot water and let the tea steep for three to five minutes before serving.

bushes and will withstand winter in milder climate zones. You will often see them as decorative hedges and shrubs in gardens throughout the Mediterranean. Mine spend the winter indoors in pots. One rosemary bush is often enough, as you don't need that much to flavor the food.

Did You Know

The most widespread herb in gardens across Norway is probably oregano, which is called mountain mint in Norwegian. It is hardy and returns year after year. In my garden, I let it grow wild, and it produces beautiful purple flowers that remind me a bit of lavender.

Growing herbs is a great activity for young and old alike, and the knowledge of herbs and their health-giving properties has been passed down from generation to generation.

PROJECT 16: MICROGREENS ALL YEAR ROUND

Pea shoots can be grown indoors all year round, are cheap, and, of course, are healthy. They have an intense flavor and are rich in nutrition and vitamins. Additionally, the shoots are often ready to harvest after just two weeks. They are great in salads and on sandwiches. It's a fun fall and winter project while you wait for the next gardening season.

Growing Pea Shoots

Grow delicious pea shoots in the kitchen window all year round. The fall and winter seasons can be tough for those of us who yearn for spring sun and sprouting seeds. Those with a real case of container garden fever are longing for the new gardening season ahead of us. There are, however, still projects you can busy yourself with even in fall and winter: you can sow peas and grow pea shoots. Wonderful to use in cooking, they make for a great winter project.

What You Will Need

Split green peas, a bowl or pot to fill with potting soil, and a window with access to daylight.

Care

The sprouts need little care, but keep the soil evenly moist and water them once a week. When it's time to harvest, cut the plant back so that the sprouts have about an inch/a couple of cm of stem left above the soil. The peas will often sprout again, and you can harvest them several times.

How

Grab a mixing bowl or pot and fill it two-thirds full with soil. Sprinkle an even layer of dried peas on the surface. Cover with a thin layer of soil (about ¾ inch/a couple of cm) and water it thoroughly. If you want faster germination, leave the dried peas

TØRKEDE GRØNNE ERTER
GRØNNE
ERTER
TØRKEDE

in water for a day before sowing them. They will then absorb some of the moisture and germinate faster.

Place the newly sown seed bowl in a warm place for the first two to three days, ideally on a warm bathroom floor. The heat leads to faster germination. Then put the bowl on a sunny windowsill and look forward to sinking your teeth into fresh, crunchy pea shoots.

Good to Know

The more light and heat, the faster the pea shoots will grow. It is therefore very easy to succeed with pea shoots from February on and in spring and summer. The darker and colder the winter, the longer it takes for the shoots to grow.

PROJECT 17: MEDITERRANEAN PLANTS

A Taste of Italy

Are you also dreaming of the Mediterranean and its hot, sunny summers, olive groves, azure waters, fig trees, and good food? Gosh, I've had so many wonderful experiences there, so it's an added delight to bring some of the Mediterranean's gorgeous atmosphere home with me. What can compare to sitting outdoors surrounded by lemon, fig, and olive trees and some fragrant lavender plants in small pots?

What You Will Need

Your selection of Mediterranean plants (see my suggestions, page 252), fairly small pots, good nutrient-rich soil (preferably formulated for Mediterranean and citrus plants), drainage aids like sand, LECA, or gravel, and plant food—either regular or citrus fertilizer, which has extra iron and magnesium.

Care

Light: Loves sunlight, but also tolerates partial shade.

Location: Ideally in a cozy, sunny corner or on a sunny terrace or balcony.

Temperature: Mediterranean plants thrive outdoors during the summer almost everywhere in Norway, as they are used to lots of sun with the odd cooler period. They can withstand a couple of frosty nights, but not long periods of freezing temperatures. They must therefore be kept indoors through the winter.

CONTAINER TIP

Do the leaves on your citrus trees turn yellow in the summer? A common reason for this is a lack of iron and magnesium in the soil. Add a Mediterranean/citrus soil blend or ericaceous compost (as a top layer over the existing soil) or, for faster results, add liquid plant food that contains a lot of iron and magnesium, for example, citrus plant food.

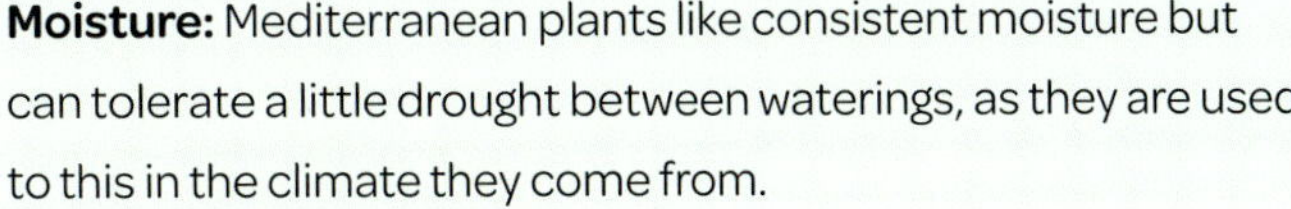

Moisture: Mediterranean plants like consistent moisture but can tolerate a little drought between waterings, as they are used to this in the climate they come from.

How

You can get that Mediterranean feeling on your balcony or in your outdoor space. How about getting a couple of Mediterranean plants, for example, an olive tree (*Olea europaea*), fig tree (*Ficus carica*), or lemon tree (*Citrus* ×*limon*)? Plant them in larger pots, ideally made of terra-cotta, which are typical in the Mediterranean. The largest trees should be placed at the back, with the smaller pots at the front. In the smaller pots, you could plant lavender, catnip, sage, or other herbs that are also typical of the Mediterranean.

You could even get yourself an outdoor bistro set, with a small table with two simple chairs, and then hang lanterns (there are so many solar-powered options here) or fairy lights around your outdoor space. Don a straw hat and pour a glass of something delicious. All there is to do then is close your eyes, feel the sun on your skin, and breathe in the scent of the Mediterranean plants around you.

How about inviting a friend over for a Mediterranean lunch with a tomato-based pasta dish garnished with herbs from your own herb garden (see page 235)? The icing on the cake would be adding your homegrown tomatoes (see page 222) too (but store-bought tomatoes are permitted).

Good to Know

Mediterranean plants do not like to sit in wet, heavy soil. You can avoid this by using well-drained soil. Mix up to one-quarter LECA, sand, or gravel into the soil when repotting. I always recommend having holes in the bottom of the pot.

When I lived in Oslo, I kept this calamondin tree (*Citrus ×microcarpa*) on the balcony in the summer and in a cool bedroom in the winter. Check out the amount of fruit on it! The calamondin is believed to be a cross between a mandarin orange and kumquat.

CONTAINER TIP

You can move your lemon tree outside in the spring. Lemon trees can handle some frost if given a chance to get used to it, but I wouldn't gamble too much on it.

It would be best to use a soil especially formulated for Mediterranean and citrus plants, which is a coarser than one formulated for flowers, and has a lower (more acid) pH. You can also use ericaceous compost or mix a little of this into ordinary potting soil. Regular potting soil often contains too much lime, which turns the leaves yellowish.

Grow Your Own Lemon Tree

Have you heard of the Amalfi lemon? It's known as the best lemon in the world and comes from the spectacular Amalfi Coast in Italy, famous for its lemon groves lining the mountainsides. Did you know that you can buy lemons, including Amalfi lemons, at the grocery store and grow your own plant from a lemon seed?

What You Will Need

Lemons (if you can get ahold of Amalfi lemons, amazing), a pot of soil (either potting soil or a blend formulated for Mediterranean or citrus plants or for flowers—I just used what I had and it seems to be going well), a clear plastic bag.

How

Cut a lemon in half and remove the seeds. Place three or four of them in moist potting soil and cover with ¾ to 1 inch/2 to 3 cm of soil. Water thoroughly. Put the pot in the plastic bag and tie it up. Put the pot somewhere warm and sunny. If there's too much moisture, make a small air hole in the plastic so that the soil doesn't get moldy. After a couple of weeks, small lemon sprouts will appear. Remove the plastic to keep mold from forming and gradually transplant the sprouts into a larger pot.

Care

As the sprouts grow, place the pot somewhere sunny and make sure that the soil doesn't dry out. Lemon trees like to be outdoors in the summer, in a greenhouse if possible. From there, you can hopefully enjoy delicious lemons in a couple of years. Mine is growing slowly but surely. FYI, I haven't had any lemons yet, but I'm keeping my fingers crossed. Good luck!

Good to Know

Lemon seeds can be sown indoors from February to March, and then be moved outside in the summer months.

Flowering citrus trees, in this case calamondin, smell heavenly, and little is more satisfying than watching the blossoms grow into gorgeous citrus fruits. I would like to say that this fruit tastes wonderful, but they are really rather sour and bitter. That's why they are better suited in a fresh summer drink.

My Mediterranean Favorites

- Fig tree (*Ficus carica*)
- Olive tree (*Olea europaea*)
- Lemon tree (*Citrus ×limon*)
- Calamondin (*Citrus ×microcarpa*)
- Myrtle (*Myrtus communis*)
- Ivy (*Hedera helix*)
- Palm trees
- Mediterranean herbs

Fig Trees

Figs are getting noticed like never before. More and more people are opening their eyes to this picture-perfect specimen of a tree. It's relatively easy to succeed with a fig tree as long as it can spend the winter indoors, although figs can also manage outdoors in the mildest areas in the Nordics.

Care

Figs need full sun to partial shade. It should be kept evenly moist; you will see the leaves close in on themselves if it hasn't received enough water. It can do well in a pot, but since the fig tree has deep roots, you should eventually repot it into a large, deep pot or cut it down if it gets too big and voluminous. Provide it with plant food once a month during the growing season.

Olive trees (*Olea europaea,* above) often lose their leaves indoors in winter if the room temperature is too high, which is most often the case in a normal temperate living room. They are best placed in a colder room during the winter, such as a bedroom. Even if the olive tree loses all its leaves, you should hold off on throwing it away. Olive trees have an impressive ability to pull through and sprout new shoots in spring and summer. Scratch at the trunk of the tree with your fingernail—if it's green underneath, there's sap, and therefore life in the tree. If you're lucky, it'll regrow again in the spring.

Potty for palms? Many palm trees are hardy and do well in pots. They tolerate dry soil between waterings and have low nutrient requirements. An easy-to-care-for plant for those of you who spend a lot of time away from home or who forget about your balcony plants every now and then. Here is my Canary Island date palm (*Phoenix canariensis,* left).

How

Figs can be easily propagated through cuttings:

- Cut off 4 to 8 inches/10 to 20 cm at the end of a branch and pluck off the lower leaves.
- It helps to cut away the very top shoot for better root growth. Remove about 1 to 1½ inches/3 to 4 cm from the top, then the cutting will redirect its energy downward to form roots, instead of sending the energy up into the top shoot.
- Stick the cutting into a pot with wet soil.
- Keep the soil evenly moist and ideally place the pot somewhere sunny.
- The plant thrives best when repotted into a larger pot during the summer.

If you're lucky, you'll have ripe figs to eat in late summer. For the fruit to grow, figs need warm temperatures and lots of sun, so putting them in a greenhouse would be advantageous. If you live somewhere cooler or where the summer is cold, don't despair, the fig tree is beautiful in itself and is a fun plant to have in your outdoor space, with or without fruit.

4

The fig has deep roots but can thrive in large pots. Here's my fig tree outside my old apartment in Oslo. Prune the tree if you want a rounder shape, and feel free to use whatever you cut off as propagation cuttings.

CONTAINER FACT

Have you heard about the Bornholm fig? A variety of fig that grows on the Danish island of the same name, it is particularly hardy and can survive the winter outdoors, despite the frosty nights. I have been lucky enough to get ahold of a cutting, which is growing quickly and which I hope to have a long relationship with. I once forgot a small fig tree in a pot under a bush in the courtyard of my apartment building back when I lived in Oslo, and even though it dropped to −4°F/−20°C that winter, it survived and even sprouted new fresh shoots in the spring.

PROJECT 18: DESIGN YOUR OWN CONTAINER GARDEN

Container plants at every height—including hanging baskets. If you have limited space on the ground or the floor of your terrace, hanging containers are a great way to utilize your space. Here, you can see our lobelia (left) in a steel hanging container and our morning glory (*Ipomoea* spp., right) in a plastic one.

Create a Living Space Outdoors with Planters and Pots

Do you dream of having a lush botanical paradise on your balcony? In a container garden, you can plant trees, perennials, ornamental grasses, and flowers, either together in larger pots or in several pots set out in wonderful harmony. By adding a small water feature, you really can get that feeling in your own private oasis.

"It's not just plants that grow and flourish in a container garden, people do too."

The most important thing when designing your own oasis is that you follow your personal taste and style. The purpose is for you to be able to relax and enjoy your container garden to the fullest. Make a plan according to what you have in the way of space, time, interest, and budget. Pots are an investment, and the nicest ones are often quite expensive, so just start with a few. Choose pots you like and that you feel go well together. Let your singular creativity guide you!

We used steel planters here to divide and build up zones in the space on our terrace. We removed the lawn in parts of the garden, lay a sheet underneath, and filled it with light gravel. This made it easier to place the boxes and create a nice, clean look, and it means that (luckily) we don't have to weed. The cozy nook created by planters and larger pots is delightful for both people and plants. And it's not just nice to have this area shaded and free of wind, it is also important for creating more sheltered areas that give your outdoor space a clearly defined zone.

What You Will Need

A small plan for the structure and composition of your container garden, a couple of your favorite pots and/or planters with your choice of plants.

How

You can build dimension in your outdoor space. With the help of large pots and planters, you can create "rooms" and divide the space.

CONTAINER TIP

Not a fan of grass lawns? You could remove parts of the lawn in your outdoor space, lay down a tarp, cover it with gravel, and place planters and pots on top. That way, you avoid weeding, and your containers will stay steady.

This box (below) is filled with catnip, as well as some hardy drought-resistant black garlic in my favorite color in the garden: PURPLE!

Pots

Stack your pots and imagine their height moving upward like a wave. Tall pots should be at the back and smaller ones up front. Place one or more larger pots at the back with some taller potted plants in them, then place a medium-sized pot and plant in the middle, and some smaller ones at the front. This then creates a lovely display for the plants, where all of them can be seen, and adds dimension to your outdoor space. Pots in different sizes, heights, and colors help create an interesting look.

"A stroll in an exclusive, small outdoor space such as a container garden filled with delightful sensory experiences lowers the heart rate and increases the quality of life."

Other decor and ornaments look great combined with containers. Small sculptures (above) can be placed next to or between the pots. A fan of garden gnomes or do you prefer more minimalist figures? Or how about a water feature nestled into your container garden? I love big colored glass bottles, such as these vintage demijohn bottles, which can also be filled with water, and you can put tall branches or flowers in them.

Want a water feature in your container garden? Yes, please. Here, we have a ceramic water mirror (opposite). Water is beautiful, provides its own sense of peace and atmosphere among your pots, and birds, insects, and other wildlife love it. Glass is beautiful to combine with pots too. Here you can see large vintage glass bottles and my grandfather's old fishing buoys.

Flower buds in a small water mirror or in a bathtub full of water, such as this steel one (opposite), make for stunning additions to the space. The flower water is great for watering your potted plants too, as it contains lots of nutrients. Pretty and useful!

Good to Know

Pots can be placed wherever you want, for example, as a way to beautify your entrance, balcony, or greenhouse. But remember that good lighting conditions—such as a couple of hours of direct sun every day—is something most plants in containers will appreciate.

PROGRESSING WITH YOUR CONTAINER GARDEN

Remember that practice makes perfect, and that you'll go a long way with some basic knowledge about water, nutrition, temperature, and choosing the best plants for your pots.

Annual flowers are for those of you keen for quick results for the summer season, *perennial plants* are for those looking for long-lasting results, *trees* are for those who love the feeling of a park in their outdoor space, and *herbs or tomatoes* for those who want to enjoy edible plants in their container. Or you could always go for a bit of everything—whatever suits your desire! With a container garden, you can easily have beautiful flowers in your outdoor space as well as delicious food that you can enjoy through the summer and fall. Even if some potted plants may die while others thrive, remember that this is precisely what makes caring for and cultivating plants so exciting. The feeling of achievement when something sprouts and thrives—you should take the moment to really enjoy it. Think of plants as friends and treat them accordingly. Surely everyone wants to be a good pal, regardless of whether that is to people, animals, or plants?

I hope that by browsing this book, you now know how creative you can get with container gardening. And, finally, I wish you the best of luck. Hope is green, as they say, green thumb or not.

PHOTO CREDITS

All photos are by author, with the exception of the following:

Astrid Waller, pages 85, 161 (bottom right), 173, 191

Belson De Coninck, pages 86 (bottom left), 98

Fredrik Bye, pages 84 (top right), 107, 217 (top), 219 (top)

Hagelandkjeden, page 44

Olaug Røyneberg, page 22

ACKNOWLEDGMENTS

Thanks to all my followers on social media who have supported my green project from the very beginning. The plant community is a peaceful and inspiring world to be a part of. Thanks also to the competent people at our literary agency, Northern Stories, who make our books travel the world and inspire readers across the globe.

REFERENCES

de Bell, S; White, M; Griffiths, A; et al. "Spending time in the garden is positively associated with health and well-being: Results from a national survey in England." *Landscape and Urban Planning.* August 2020. Summary.

Hunter, MCR; Gillespie, BW; Yu-Pu Chen, S. "Urban Nature Experiences Reduce Stress in the Context of Daily Life Based on Salivary Biomarkers." *Frontiers in Psychology.* 2019. frontiersin.org

Spilled, Ingrid. "Those Who Used the Garden Reported Better Health." *Frontiers in Psychology.* May 2020. forskning.no/forebyggende-helse/de-som-brukte-hagenreported-about-better-health/1683248

INDEX

D

E

F

M

N

O

P

R

S

Anders Røyneberg, known as the @arcticgardener on Instagram, is an agronomist, plant lover, psychiatric nurse, and sexologist. For his day job, Anders works as a therapist, writer, and lecturer and can often be seen on *Good Morning Norway*, where he offers cultivation inspiration and shares the joy of gardening. Together with Erik Schjerven, he has previously published the bestsellers *The Joyful Gardener*, *Plant Bonanza*, and *Green Home*, which have collectively been translated into ten languages.

Translation by Megan Turney and Quarto Translations

All photos taken by the author. Other photo and illustration credits appear on page 270.

Timber Press
Workman Publishing
Hachette Book Group, Inc.
1290 Avenue of the Americas
New York, New York 10104
timberpress.com

Timber Press is an imprint of Workman Publishing, a division of Hachette Book Group, Inc. The Timber Press name and logo are registered trademarks of Hachette Book Group, Inc.

Printed in Shenzhen, China (APO), on responsibly sourced paper
Text and cover design by Nami Kurita

ISBN 978-1-64326-539-1

A catalog record for this book is available from the Library of Congress.